TOUGH TUCKER CARLSON

AMERICA'S TRUTH WARRIOR

DAVID LYNCH

BLENHEIM PRESS LLC

For Nancy, Scott, Bridget, and Colleen. I still love all of you more than horseradish.

CONTENTS

Tough Tucker Carlson: America's Truth Warrior

Published by Blenheim Press LLC
Cleveland, OH

Paperback ISBN: 979-8-9888535-9-6
Hardcover ISBN: 979-8-9888535-8-9

BIOGRAPHY & AUTOBIOGRAPHY / Political

BLENHEIM PRESS LLC

FOREWORD

Tucker Carlson's career has been surprising when you look at the way he started. He actually didn't even begin with the idea of being a writer or a public figure of any sort.

Right out of college he applied for a job with the Central Intelligence Agency in Langley, Virginia. He saw his future in the world of spies and gathering secret intelligence. Even as a college student and history major, Carlson was a good writer who thought this skill could help him prepare reports and dossiers important for those that protect this great country that he loves.

When the CIA turned him down flat, they sent Tucker Carlson off in a completely different direction that ultimately led him to serve his country through a fearless desire to deliver important truths to his fellow citizens.

Tucker's disappointment in his inability to fulfill his patriotic ambitions through spycraft led him to a different kind of patriotic service for which this writer continues to be grateful.

CHAPTER 1
SUDDEN FIRING

E verybody in media knew about Carlson's TV show. Through the years he had broken many important stories and his famous writing ability brought him to this point where he was in great demand. Guests yearned for the opportunity to appear on television with the erudite Carlson.

He was especially well known in the Los Angeles area where fame and notoriety were at a premium, assuring the best tables at the most expensive restaurants where the maître d' would fawn over the news man. Carlson was always on the "A" guest list for those interested in throwing a glitzy cocktail party.

Carlson's success in television came with a lot of other perks. People listened to what he had to say even at the grocery store or the local fast food establishment. Life was good.

When he signed off the air on Friday he told his loyal viewers that he would be back on Monday to present more of the beloved Carlson commentary on the issues of the day.

Carlson made a few notes on Saturday as a beginning outline of the production going on the air on Monday. He called the clothier who was paid by the network to make sure that all of his suits had that impeccable look commensurate with his status as the most sophisticated news guy around.

Carlson wasn't really the kind of egotist who wanted special treatment, but he did love the fact that the television producers paid for the beautiful suits including alterations by Hollywood's most sophisticated tailor so that his pants could have that perfect crease every time he went before the cameras.

He called the shop and told them that he would pick up his suits in an hour. The proprietor told him that the suits would not be ready because of a call received from the TV producer.

What?

The store owner then informed Carlson that he had been canceled and that Carlson's program would not be airing on Monday.

In other words, they were told to hold off on the gorgeous Carlson garments because the network would no longer pay for them.

Carlson was stunned. He told the shopkeeper to get the outfits ready because Carlson himself would pay the tab.

In the meantime, Carlson was shocked. He'd had disagreements with the people in charge before but never anticipated that they would suddenly pull the plug on his popular program. Especially without telling him first.

Carlson contacted his family and told them what happened. He then contemplated his future.

Thus was the life of the popular news guru named Richard Carlson. The year was 1973.

He had dinner that night with his young family. Four-year-old Tucker gave his dad a sweet smile and said, "it'll be okay, daddy."

And oh my, Tucker Carlson was certainly right about that.

Richard "Dick" Carlson was intense and a great talk show host. Tucker inherited the wavy hair.

CHAPTER 2
UKRAINE

On February 27, 2022 Utah Senator Mitt Romney appeared with CNN correspondent Dana Bash and issued the following stunning paraphrased proclamation:

The Russian invasion of Ukraine places the free world in an epic showdown between despotism and the American tradition of freedom. People who ask America not to intervene on behalf of the Ukrainian people almost commit treason against the American government. Fox News commentator Tucker Carlson has taken up the defense of Vladimir Putin and therefore has come close to committing the crime of treason against the United States of America.

This amazing statement by former presidential candidate Mitt Romney rocked America from one coastline to another. Throughout the media world, political commentators trembled in the face of these stunning accusations against Fox News host Tucker Carlson.

American media figures were afraid: criticism of

Senator Mitt Romney saw Carlson's skepticism over Ukraine spending as treasonous.

America's involvement in the protection of Ukraine forces was tamped down. Everyone in the broadcast and cable television world feared the idea that open discussion of the American response in Ukraine would result in the FBI banging down the doors of the commentators and dragging them off to a federal holding facility.

Even Tucker Carlson's associates in the Fox Newsroom were reticent in the face of the harsh attacks from Senator Romney.

In many media circles, such as MSNBC and *The Washington Post*, newsrooms repeated the accusations of treason against Carlson. Eventually other members of Congress and members of the Biden administration joined in the chorus asking that something be done about Carlson's allegedly treasonous remarks.

The pressure on Rupert Murdoch's Fox News Corporation was withering. The London-based Murdoch empire was besieged with emails, phone calls, and social media posts demanding Carlson be pulled off the air as a man who was acting in an anti-American fashion in opposing the American war effort on behalf of the poor Ukrainian people.

The New York Times described Carlson as a criminal, saying that he used his lofty perch at Fox News to give aid and comfort to our enemies in the Russian regime. They asked that Tucker be punished in the same way we punished spies who stole our nuclear secrets in the post-World War II era because Carlson was an enemy of the people.

The vilification of one man in the face of a patriotic call for war had not been seen on this scale since Charles Lindbergh urged President Roosevelt to resist plans to have the United States join the war against the Nazis and Adolf Hitler.

But even Lindbergh was defended by some in the American press who recognized that Lindbergh's isolationist philosophy was a legitimate viewpoint subject to open discussion. Many thought that Lindbergh was dead wrong and history shows that his judgment was ill advised.

Despite this, no one contemplated the idea that Lindbergh should be silenced and perhaps even imprisoned for expressing his viewpoint. The American media in 1940 still recognized that the First Amendment required open discussion of American war policy, even if some viewpoints were considered outrageously inconsistent with American interests.

The situation regarding Tucker Carlson in June of 2022 however was truly unique. Never before had leaders so universally condemned a news commentator. Never before had the entire American media structure demanded prosecution of a journalist as a traitor.

As incredible as the situation was, even more incredible was the Tucker Carlson response.

Carlson doubled down in his public pronouncements, asking for more debate on the topic of American involvement in Ukraine. Carlson argued that spending billions of tax dollars to defend the Ukrainian government that itself was showing signs of totalitarianism was if not a mistake at least the kind of thing that demanded an extensive floor debate in Congress and extensive discussion in the public square.

Carlson was being punished for merely asking that American citizens pause to think about the wisdom of this huge expenditure in a time of severe inflation especially when the Ukrainian regime used its military to silence dissent of its own citizens.

Carlson refused to back down in his steadfast insistence on further discussion and evaluation. He showed incredible courage given the pressure from American government officials and the pressure from Carlson's bosses at the Fox News Corporation.

Just who was this public figure named Tucker Carlson who was willing to stand up as a voice in the wilderness against these unending accusations of treason?

The journey of Tucker Carlson to reach this point in his career and his historic courage in the middle of the Ukrainian war drumbeat is both fascinating and inspiring.

This book traces the life of Tucker Carlson as the leading voice of conservative expression in America and demonstrates how his life brought him to this moment of courage that would set the tone for the discussion of American policy for decades to come.

Essentially, Tucker Carlson has emerged as a hero for free speech at a time when cancel culture threatens to silence those who have thoughts independent from the plans of government.

Carlson carries the torch of free expression forward today using *Twitter* as his platform.

The effort to prevent free thought expressed passionately out loud has been marching forward over the last several years.

Tucker Carlson stands in the breach to stop this march and preserve the First Amendment. This is his story.

CHAPTER 3
TUCKER LIFE

Tucker Carlson was born in San Francisco in 1969 and had a somewhat unsettled youth.

His mother was Lisa McNear, an artist who was always trying to "find herself" through exploration of artistic trends. Seven years after Tucker's birth, she walked out on the family, leaving six-year-old Tucker and his four-year-old brother to build a new life with his father Dick Carlson. Dick Carlson was a shrewd political operator and savvy media manager. He parlayed his connections to become Director of the Voice of America. In 1991, President George H.W. Bush then appointed Dick Carlson ambassador to the Seychelles, a tropical island republic in the western Indian Ocean.

After two years in the embassy, he ascended to the presidency of PBS, where he became a fierce defender of the government's funding of public broadcasting as a source of neutral reportage free of political influence.

Dick Carlson became a champion of dynamic "truth to power" journalism as he directed coverage of the Tiananmen

Square rebellion in China at a time when the federal government was courting enhanced U.S.-China relations. Carlson helped give a voice to liberty in the face of crackdowns on dissent in Beijing.

Dick Carlson was awarded custody of both boys, not surprising as Tucker's mother pursued the bohemian lifestyle of a roaming artist, frequently finding her muse in cocaine and marijuana induced trips to beautiful states of artistic awareness.

The court may have seen father Dick Carlson as providing a significantly more stable environment life in comparison to the hippie wanderlust of his mother, but life with father was not ideal in terms of making a close knit family unit.

Dick Carlson's fast-paced type A career left little time for family dinners and bedtime stories. As a result, Tucker and his brother experienced a boarding school existence where a good night kiss and a hug would forever be impossible. As dad worked the political cocktail party circuit, the two little boys were forced to grow up in dormitories attached to expensive preparatory schools surrounded by other lonely progeny of the privileged.

Tucker Carlson

Grainy photo from Carlson's grade school yearbook. The famous Tucker Carlson hair was already in full bloom.

So for the most part, Tucker was raised by caring on-campus proctors who did their best to fill the void created by the absence of a normal family routine.

Tucker's mother made no real effort to be present in her son's life, forming a live-in relationship with British sculptor Mo McDermott.

McDermott died of alcoholism in 1988 and Tucker's mom then married British painter Michael Vaughn with whom she traveled between homes in France and South Carolina. Tucker's mom died in 2011 estranged from her two boys, leaving a large inheritance but not to her two sons. Lawyers interceded and the Tucker boys were awarded large sums by the probate court in 2019. Tucker's mother also left memorable artistic projects as a testament to her artistic vision.

Dick Carlson's highflying lifestyle was easily supported by generous salaries but the Tucker boys and their father reached a rare level of wealthy living when Dick Carlson remarried. His new bride in 1979 was Swanson TV dinner heiress Patricia Swanson.

The three men of the Carlson family would never again worry about money. They now breathed the rarefied air of the super-rich. Dick Carlson was however no gold-digger lazing around in the lap of luxury. Patricia Swanson admired the take-no-prisoners media manager who worked 70 hours a week in pursuit of truth and integrity in reporting on international affairs. Dick Carlson was a high achiever and Pat Swanson loved her white knight hero.

Tucker Carlson might have been a boarding school brat but being forced to make it by himself without a meaningful parental relationship made him tough and motivated him to reach his goals in his own way and on his own terms.

He was forced to grow up fast and keep his own counsel. Living away from home through all of grade school, high school, and college, he emerged from Trinity College with a degree in history, ready to forge his own pathway.

After graduation, he eschewed the idea of using his wealth as a passport to a cushy executive position. The CIA rejected his application. He then chose to start at the bottom rung of the ladder to pursue a career in journalism.

He began as a lowly fact checker for the *Policy Review* and then wrote editorials for the *Arkansas Democrat Gazette* in Little Rock. Not exactly the top of the journalistic food chain, but he had faith in himself, and he was paying his dues. He moved on to help inaugurate the *Weekly Standard*, a conservative periodical created by Bill Kristol (today an ardent anti-Trumper).

Carlson's career took flight after he interviewed George W. Bush for *Talk Magazine*. The published interview caused a huge stir.

It quoted the presidential wannabe using very coarse language and even painted the younger Bush as finding humor in Texas's liberal use of the death penalty. Carlson's *Talk Magazine* interview with Bush nearly derailed the younger Bush's candidacy.

However, it rocketed Carlson into the national spotlight. He was now a nationally known commodity.

He then bounced between various national publications, remaining on the radar screen for the reading public. The reading public, however, was still a somewhat limited audience.

The lion's share of public attention by this time was not focused on print. The big game was now electronic media: television, radio, and the Internet. Printed copy was fading from the scene: the big stars in journalism were in front of a video camera.

Although he was winning awards for outstanding thoughtful articles in *Esquire* and *The Wall Street Journal*, he remained a backbencher to television commentators capturing the American imagination.

CHAPTER 4
TV COMES CALLING

National television networks were expanding in the early 2000's, with Fox, CNN, MSNBC, TBS, and a myriad of other cable networks giving the big three broadcast companies a run for their money. Political commentary on TV was exploding and these new news networks scoured the country looking for new talent to fill the broadcast day.

National news publications served as the training ground for television, and producers began to sign up writers who could talk coherently on cable. Tucker, always articulate, was perfect for the medium of cable television.

Cable TV allowed for longform discussions never found on the broadcast networks of NBC, ABC, and CBS. This was tailor-made for the history major with a great writing resume. It also didn't hurt that his dad was a legend in the industry.

In 2000, Carlson co-hosted *The Spin Room* on CNN. In 2001 he co-hosted *Crossfire* also on CNN, playing the role of the designated conservative debating the designated liberal often in the person of outspoken Clintonite James Carville.

In 2004, Carlson was rocked by the *Daily Show's* Jon

Stewart who appeared under the pretense of promoting his new book on *Crossfire*. Instead, he launched into an attack of Carlson claiming his style of right-wing apologetics was harmful to political discourse in America.

A Young Tucker begins his TV journey.

Carlson snapped back at Stewart's leftist bias, clearly upset with the Stewart ambush. The *New York Times* called the Stewart appearance an "ignominious career moment" for Carlson.

This was an exaggeration. Carlson remained professional under fire. Shortly thereafter, CNN canceled Carlson's contract. Carlson later said he had planned to leave *Crossfire* long before Stewart's attack, but clearly Carlson's approach to his TV appearances was shifting.

In 2005, before his *Crossfire* departure, Carlson hosted *Tucker Carlson Unfiltered* which ran on PBS while he was making his CNN appearances. Tucker was on two networks at the same time.

In June 2005 Carlson left both CNN and PBS to debut *Tucker* on MSNBC featuring a dynamic new personality, Rachel Maddow, on a regular basis. Maddow became a rising star at MSNBC and soon she became the flagship voice for the network as it moved further left in philosophy.

By the time 2008 rolled around, MSNBC had become a virtual campaign outpost for the Democratic Party. Tucker felt completely out of place.

Tucker was canceled in March 2008, and he was relieved. MSNBC didn't want him anymore, a square peg unable to fit in the round hole socialistic MSNBC agenda.

Carlson also realized that somehow he had screwed up his own media persona during his television career. He needed to find his core self and let it shine. The real Tucker Carlson had become buried as he played this role like an actor.

He was scripted as the white shoe Ivy League conservative playing tennis at the exclusive country club. And while he played the role well, it wasn't who he really was. It wasn't the real Tucker.

The real Tucker hungered to tell the truth. He resented being marched out to defend Bush White House policies aimed at regime change in the Middle East. He realized that he was becoming a spokesman for the military industrial complex.

He was defending wars created to keep the defense industry in the chips. And often at the expense of American lives.

Yes, his father had played the political game but dear old dad would not have compromised important truths on the altar of political expedience. And comforting the wealthy made him uncomfortable despite his own pretty elitist upbringing.

Tucker was ready to dedicate himself to telling the truth only, all else be damned. The kid who had to make his own way as a youth was prepared to do something to save his own soul. Cracks in the fake country club Republican facade that Tucker had maintained began to appear in 2006.

DAVID LYNCH

That's when Tucker abandoned his bowtie. That bowtie was emblematic of Republicans who sold out Republican ideals and favored the good old boy system where war was good for business.

In 2006, Tucker tossed the bowtie in favor of the standard half-windsor knot typical for TV talking heads. The pretense was gone. Tucker was leaving the big business Republican reservation. And finally, after his departure from MSNBC in 2008, Tucker was ready for a metamorphosis.

He couldn't play act anymore in this Republican Party game that lied to the people.

He wanted to sleep at night. He wanted to live in the light of truth. He allowed himself to be himself. The new Tucker was ready but was American television ready? Ready for this new man? This resurrected zealot of truth?

The emergence of the real Tucker Carlson, however, didn't happen without some stutter steps.

The new arch-conservative Tucker Carlson was like a mighty oak that would only take root on just the right mixture of soil and fertile ground. Tucker was ready but he was unable to find the right forum. He was a true believer in American exceptionalism.

He was a man with a speech to give but with no stage on which he was welcome to give it. Fox news, Rupert Murdoch's cable behemoth, seemed a logical choice and Fox liked the cut of his jib. Carlson then officially joined the Fox News team.

However, Fox executives also felt that Carlson, despite his already impressive cable resume, was not ready for prime time. And they were right.

Carlson seemed tentative and unsure of his own identity in 2009. He was finally on the right network, Fox news

Corporation. Unfortunately, he needed more seasoning in the transformational stage. There was an authentic Tucker Carlson inside ready to proclaim his truth. But Tucker at this stage was searching for the right mode of expression to let the lion out of his cage.

He was still outwardly clinging to a highbrow condescending persona that was ill-suited to the straightforward approach needed to reveal the populist that had been developing in him over the years. He knew the real truth of RINO (Republican in Name Only) hypocrisy by this time, but he had not yet figured out the way to reveal his true identity.

Fox news saw this but remained unsure of his ability to fight in the heavyweight division of cable news. For this reason, Fox moved Carlson all around the TV schedule where he discharged his duties in a workmanlike fashion.

They liked him but didn't love him. Carlson was like that great utility player on a major-league baseball roster. He does well when they insert him in the lineup but went back to the bench when the frontline player recovered from injuries.

Tucker knew that if given the right chance he could be more than a utility player. He had what it took to be an All-Star but he needed an opportunity to be in the everyday lineup to show people the stuff he was made of.

In the meantime, Tucker went into the regular rotation of Fox News contributors bouncing from show to show in spot appearances on an as-needed basis.

Fox News always keeps a stable of talking heads, each paid a retainer to make an appearance at the drop of a hat to help fill out the long list of hour-long shows that populate the Fox News' nightly schedule.

Being a Fox News contributor is a lucrative part-time gig.

The key to success is being ready to drop everything and perform on cue in a very brief segment.

Continuing with the baseball analogy, a Fox News contributor was a pinch-hitter who had to be ready when the coach tells you to come off the bench and grab a bat.

The pay is great, somewhere between $100,000 a year for rookies and close to $500,000 for regular guests who speak with authority. Occasionally, a Fox News contributor will guest-host for one of the nightly stars who anchor their own programs.

If this happens, you look for the day when you get the call to host your own show. Those guest host performances are critiqued by Fox News leadership trying to discover the next big thing in cable news. When you guest host, you are auditioning for something bigger.

The reigning champion at Fox in those days was Bill O'Reilly. *The O'Reilly Factor* owned nighttime cable by a wide margin. Some nights O'Reilly had a larger audience than all the other cable news channels combined.

O'Reilly had been a knock-around TV news reporter before he was crowned king over at Fox. He had an impatient personality not suffering fools lightly, creating what he called *The No Spin Zone* where hypocrites and fakers would be exposed and then verbally flogged by O'Reilly.

O'Reilly exuded confidence as he dismantled progressive Democrats and went on tirade after tirade.

O'Reilly's forceful personality jumped out at you from your television set. As the years went by O'Reilly's ratings and domineering personality attracted sponsors with millions in advertising.

The advertisers realized that O'Reilly's audience had developed an almost religious fervor for this primetime cable host. O'Reilly's millions of fans trusted him implicitly and would buy the products hawked during commercial breaks.

O'Reilly was a fearless leader of conservative stalwarts embracing conservative ideals on national TV. Fox's many conservatives on Fox News and O'Reilly were an oasis of courageous broadcasting in a wasteland of liberal television.

All the major TV broadcast networks and almost all the other cable channels had been skewing left of center for years and now finally O'Reilly became the voice of reason, challenging the mainstream flow.

O'Reilly and Fox were riding very high in the saddle at the time Tucker Carlson joined the Fox team as a bit player.

However, Tucker realized that Fox just might be the place where he could feel at home being himself, finally. He told himself to be patient. The right time for him would materialize eventually.

He waited.

CHAPTER 5
FALL OF THE KING

B ill O'Reilly's path to the top of cable broadcasting was a little more traditional than that of his successor Tucker Carlson. O'Reilly, born in 1949, was a tall athletic Irish kid from the hardscrabble town of Levittown, New York.

His height and athleticism were imposing, and his real talent led to a role as a star pitcher for the semi-pro *New York Monarchs*. Unfortunately, his skills were just not enough for a career in the majors, so he began to direct his energies in a more traditional direction.

After graduating with a B.A. in history from Marist College, he taught high school English for two years in Miami, Florida. He wasn't happy with life as a teacher. He was restless, searching for his niche in life.

He then went for his Master's degree, this time in broadcast journalism from Boston University, working part-time as a reporter for various newspapers, even interning at WBZ-TV in Boston.

He was ready for a TV career but hesitated. In 1995 he

obtained a Masters degree from the John F. Kennedy School of Government at Harvard University.

He loved to talk and sometimes even to pontificate. He was opinionated. The Harvard degree pointed him toward a career in government and perhaps even politics.

After all, he was witty, glib, handsome, tall, with an authoritative baritone voice. An Irish Catholic with all this talent and a degree from the JFK School of Government seemed a natural to follow in the tradition of the Kennedy clan. Bill O'Reilly was poised for a life in politics.

But O'Reilly still had the bug for TV news, and he had to follow his heart. Like so many before and after him, he began with local news, cutting his teeth at various affiliates, moving up in the world from the small to medium markets, getting rave reviews wherever he landed.

Highly respected CBS News made the up-and-coming O'Reilly an international correspondent who covered big events in Central America. He was CBS's go-to guy in coverage of the brief Falkland Islands war, and he was dynamic. O'Reilly had his own film crew and was clearly destined for the national scene.

O'Reilly was a swaggering take-no-prisoners intrepid story seeker at this time and he and his camera crew broke many important stories. O'Reilly though was principled and more importantly was no pushover. When another bigger CBS correspondent stole credit for footage O'Reilly had suffered to obtain, O'Reilly stood his ground. He told his CBS bosses to give his team credit for the footage or watch him quit.

They watched him quit.

CBS would not relent, and O'Reilly kept his word,

heading to the exits in protest. Those who knew the sometimes-hotheaded Irishman weren't surprised. He did not suffer deceit lightly, even if the deceit came from the Tiffany network where he hoped to be the next Edward R. Murrow or even the next Walter Cronkite.

But talent always rises to the top. He was soon winning awards for ABC news after catching the attention of the legendary Roone Arledge, the creator of *The Wide World of Sports* and the man who saved ABC News. O'Reilly was now getting regular spots all over ABC.

While he wasn't hosting, he was impressing with quick hits on *Nightline* and *Good Morning America*. *King World*, the monstrous syndication company, lured O'Reilly to a lucrative production post for *Inside Edition*, a gossipy one-hour daily news program where he eventually became the popular anchor of this somewhat fluffy show that had terrific ratings.

Inside Edition was great for O'Reilly's career and his national profile. But O'Reilly tired of the tabloid tone. O'Reilly rightly saw himself as a hard news guy.

He was anxious to sink his teeth into important stories and he left *Inside Edition* to see if the hard-charging newsman in him could get back on track.

In 1996, the chairman of Fox News, Roger Ailes, had an idea that the outspoken O'Reilly had an everyman quality that would draw viewers to the hard-hitting style that O'Reilly longed to put on display on a national platform.

O'Reilly saw his opportunity and made the most of it. Fox News did not have the audience of the big three networks and didn't even have the heft of CNN on cable.

The O'Reilly Factor out of the box was attacking controversial topics each show frequently featuring a confrontation between O'Reilly and a left-wing ideologue. O'Reilly's audience grew quickly, O'Reilly describing himself as an independent who was "looking out for the folks".

His independence was genuine: he wasn't always towing the line when it came to Republican conservatism. He admitted that he tilted right but lambasted Neocons and RINOS who abandoned the patriotic spirit of Ronald Reagan in favor of pursuing money and reelection above the nation's interest.

He frequently complained that there were few differences between Republicans and Democrats, both parties accommodating each other instead of standing up for their core values. And he hit hard when he sensed dissembling and evasiveness in the face of direct questions.

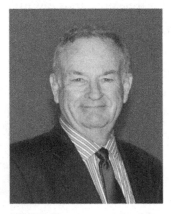

Bill O'Reilly was arrogant and confident, but had unprecedented success in the ratings

The confrontations made headlines, and this ginned up the ratings. One such confrontation, with Congressman Barney Frank, Democrat of Maryland, went viral, O'Reilly yelling at the top of his lungs, calling Frank a hypocrite.

It was mesmerizing television and Roger Ailes saw that O'Reilly was taking the 8 O'clock prime time slot to new heights. By September 2009 the *O'Reilly Factor* was the highest rated cable news show and the audience continued to grow.

O'Reilly's sometimes condescending style emanated from the self-confidence that viewers liked. Through it all, O'Reilly managed to convey that his tough-guy persona was needed to protect and represent the common man in America.

He was a tough kid from Levittown that would not let down the folks from the old neighborhood, folks frequently left out in the cold when fake conservative Republicans made backroom deals with far-left Democrats.

O'Reilly was by now a threat to the big three networks with his phenomenal ratings.

O'Reilly was so popular that he was elevated to cultural icon, spoofed on *Saturday Night Live* and by late-night comics. Amazingly, O'Reilly reveled in the attacks from mainstream media.

O'Reilly appeared on *The View*, the left-wing feminists talk show. He exchanged appearances with Stephen Colbert and even made several appearances on Jon Stewart's *The Daily Show* where he had several verbal boxing matches with the satirist.

O'Reilly frequently came off smug and off-balance on these other shows, but his ratings increased. It seems O'Reilly was finding new viewers by venturing out from the land of Fox News and into liberal ABC, CBS, and *Comedy Central* territory. This drove the anti-O'Reilly crowd insane.

It seemed that O'Reilly could do no wrong. Then came the year 2017, O'Reilly comfortably perched atop the news show ratings totem pole.

That year the *New York Times* began reporting on various allegations of sexual harassment against O'Reilly. Evidence of multimillion dollar settlements paid to various female accusers was made public.

The damage to the Fox reputation was severe, especially since O'Reilly's boss Roger Ailes had recently departed Fox under the cloud of anchor Gretchen Carlson's (no relation to Tucker) sex abuse suit against Ailes.

Fox settled the Gretchen Carlson claim, but the torrent of O'Reilly sex claims was too much for Fox owner Rupert Murdoch to bear.

O'Reilly's problems were especially galling in light of O'Reilly's frequently "holier than thou" attitude. O'Reilly had appointed himself a moral authority simultaneous to acting immorally with Fox beauties in the newsroom.

Murdoch surmised that the sexual revelations would chase away O'Reilly's viewers, so why not take control now and pull the plug instead of enduring a slow death. O'Reilly was terminated by Murdoch by way of a phone call from his London office.

The king of cable news was dead. Now what?

Tucker Carlson was far from the obvious choice.

Fox fans speculated that Sean Hannity, a longtime Fox commentator, would be moved up into the golden prime time 8 o'clock spot. Hannity had solid gold conservative credentials and a big audience that included many aficionados of his daily syndicated radio program.

But Murdoch liked to leave talent in their already established timeslots. He didn't like to upset viewer patterns, preferring to plug something new into a vacancy rather than reshuffle the entire lineup.

The world waited for white smoke from Murdoch's London headquarters to signal a decision.

Murdoch landed on Tucker Carlson. Many industry leaders thought at first that this must've been a mistake.

Carlson after all was just a role player at Fox. Most importantly, he lacked the conservative street cred to take the place of O'Reilly. Carlson was viewed as a white shoe establishment Republican, the kind despised by O'Reilly.

How could preppy Ivy league Carlson fill the spot formerly occupied by the man that hated institutional elite Republicans? Especially since Carlson seemed like the embodiment of a hoity-toity Bush family dynasty conservative.

Murdoch forged ahead with Tucker Carlson despite the criticism from O'Reilly devotees who felt betrayed. Fox at 8 o'clock was a no spin and no BS zone. How could the product of exclusive private schools replace the tough scrapper from Levittown?

The world would have to wait and see.

But Carlson did not wait long to let the viewers know that what they were getting had undergone a transformation over the last few years.

That transformation was complete by the time Murdoch handed him the O'Reilly slot.

In fact, although Carlson was born into wealth and lived the 1% lifestyle, he had adopted the values of Bill O'Reilly. Carlson's disgust over the trickery and warmongering from the Bush Republicans had made him more Levittown than Hyannis Port. People just didn't know it yet.

Tucker Carlson was also smart. He had followed O'Reilly closely and admired O'Reilly's populist pluck. Much more importantly however, Carlson crossed over to become a true believer in the O'Reilly skepticism over big government and he winced at the way big media ignored important stories.

Tucker was determined to take the O'Reilly approach and turn up the heat even further on uncomfortable Republicans and the mainstream talking heads who covered for government officials.

O'Reilly was gone but Tucker Carlson was going to increase the effort to break new stories ignored not only by the networks but also ignored even by other Fox News programs. Carlson was going to light a fuse to a rocket that would either ascend to new heights or just explode into a fiery failure.

CHAPTER 6
O'REILLY ON STEROIDS

Tucker *Carlson Tonight* took over O'Reilly's 8 o'clock hour in April of 2017 and they hit the ground running.

In fact, Carlson had already perfected the structure of his program and had a well-trained team on board by the time he was handed the reins of that choice 8 PM prime time position.

Tucker was ready to launch into his own brand of television journalism because Fox had actually given him his own one-hour program previously by penciling him in in the 7 PM slot just ahead of O'Reilly back in November of 2016 right after Donald Trump was elected president.

Then in January of 2017, Megan Kelly signed a lucrative agreement with NBC leaving the 9 PM slot at Fox open. Tucker was quickly moved from the 7 PM slot to the 9 PM slot and Carlson continued to hone his skills and sharpen his program.

With O'Reilly's sudden and somewhat shocking departure in April of 2017, Carlson's takeover of the 8 o'clock show meant that O'Reilly's successor had been given plenty of time to work out the kinks of his program. He gained valuable experience by occupying the 7 PM and later the 9 PM positions.

Most importantly, Carlson used these few months in the lower profile part of the schedule to establish a rhythm for his program and used this experience to establish a rapport with his staff and to establish a routine in the way that the program was to develop each hour.

This was a great advantage for Carlson and for Fox because they were not dropping a bunch of greenhorns into the most cherished cable broadcast position in the world. When Tucker took over from O'Reilly, he had already found his voice and the right producers and directors to put his own stamp on his program.

Megyn Kelly's departure for greener pastures was the first domino that had to fall to lead Tucker to prime time. Next came the fall of O'Reilly, and before you knew it, Carlson was batting cleanup.

In other words, when Carlson took over from O'Reilly, it was a turnkey operation ready to go.

Tucker had been creating and was now about to find a larger audience for his own kind of program formed by his own personality. Tucker continued using his slogan: **The program that is the sworn enemy of lying, pomposity, smugness, and groupthink.**

O'Reilly had put a stamp on his show as **The No Spin Zone.**

O'Reilly wanted the world to know that nobody could come on his program and spread a bunch of BS. O'Reilly would not allow officials to "spin".

The Carlson slogan was more personal. While O'Reilly

didn't want anyone handing him a bunch of baloney on the air, Carlson's slogan included his opposition to pomposity. Although Carlson like O'Reilly wouldn't tolerate lying, Carlson wanted to put a stop to leaders who use a condescending tone typical for the ruling elites in Washington.

In other words, Carlson was a little bit edgier than O'Reilly in seeking the truth. Carlson found that politicians not only lie but frequently emphasize their superiority in telling those lies.

O'Reilly's interviews and program structure were always built around O'Reilly as the wisecracking hero taking down bureaucrats who were victimizing the little guy.

Carlson's program was immediately different because Carlson did not have to be the hero. Carlson always seemed more focused on the subject matter and the facts. He never showed the arrogance and over-the-top screaming typical of O'Reilly when he smelled blood.

This more self-effacing style of Tucker Carlson won viewers over immediately, especially when Carlson detected pomposity, that characteristic that Tucker most detested.

O'Reilly wanted viewers to conclude that O'Reilly was rescuing the common man from governmental or corporate abuse. Carlson also went after abuse but never in a way that portrayed Carlson in a heroic light.

Carlson was calm but persistent in confronting pompous asses with cold hard facts and data and then letting the truth speak for itself.

The Carlson method was to allow himself to be the conduit for truth without taking credit for it. This technique was actually more palatable for viewers in comparison to the

O'Reilly style. Almost from the beginning Carlson began matching O'Reilly's fantastic ratings.

In just a few months after Carlson ascended to the 8 o'clock throne, his television ratings were surpassing O'Reilly's and the numbers began to grow exponentially, pouring more and more dollars into Murdoch coffers.

Tucker's version of the 8 o'clock hour had one other feature superior to the O'Reilly show. It was apparent from the beginning that Tucker Carlson's program was driven more by data and research than the O'Reilly program. O'Reilly was much more interested in loud confrontations.

Carlson was backed up by overwhelming research supplying the host with hordes of data frequently converted into charts and graphics that bolstered his arguments. In some ways, Carlson in this regard was more intellectual than O'Reilly and was shooting for a more educated audience that would understand his statistical analyses.

This was much more effective in counter pointing against a guest in comparison to the O'Reilly bluster.

It was clear that Carlson was youthfully dynamic in comparison to O'Reilly and that Carlson was supported by an equally youthful aggressive staff providing him with accurate argument-winning data.

And it did not take long for the Fox leadership to realize that the O'Reilly program had become worn and dated, especially in comparison to the slick fast-moving well researched *Tucker Carlson Tonight* show.

Audiences were enthralled. The Carlson show successfully retained all the aging baby boomers that loved O'Reilly. But Carlson added a younger demographic looking for a more professional data driven experience.

Before long, *Tucker Carlson Tonight* became a phenomenon

dominating cable news in a way that made O'Reilly seem like a distant memory of a long gone era. Tucker Carlson was succeeding in a way that surpassed the O'Reilly years.

The new King of prime-time cable television was now ready to expand his kingdom.

CHAPTER 7
AMAZING DAD

After learning about all the ups and downs of Tucker Carlson's career and the courageous way in which he has gone against the grain of mainstream media, you have to admit that one adjective that applies to Tucker Carlson is the word **resilient.**

If you were to ask Tucker Carlson the source of this resilience, it's likely that he would say that he gets it from his father.

Richard Warner Carlson.

The life of Tucker Carlson's father reads like a *Horatio Alger* story. His humble roots are enough to make you cry and that just adds to the admiration you have for the man considering what he was able to achieve.

Dorothy Anderson was only 15 years old and a junior in high school when her love affair with the handsome college student Richard Boynton resulted in a pregnancy that Dorothy was desperate to keep secret as long as possible.

She was able to hide the pregnancy from her mom and dad for quite a long time by wearing loose fitting clothes and also by starving herself in order to slow the baby's development.

But before long, she couldn't keep this secret from her parents who helped her through the final stages of the pregnancy while also making sure that the rest of the world did not know what was going on. The newly born Richard Boynton was a sickly baby because of Dorothy's lack of nutrition during the pregnancy.

The child was given to *The Home For Little Wanderers* in Boston, Massachusetts in hopes that a kind adoptive family could be found. In the meantime, the baby's father Richard Boynton wanted Dorothy to reclaim the child from the orphanage and elope with him.

Dorothy wanted none of this and instead chose to finish her education and allow *The Little Wanderers Home* to find a good family for placement of baby Richard. Boynton was crestfallen when he realized that Dorothy had moved on and that the three of them would never be a family. A few days later, the baby's father shot and killed himself in a fit of melancholy.

The orphanage finally found a foster family who cared for the boy for two years until an adoption could be arranged. During this period, Dorothy would visit her little son at the foster parents without telling anyone that she was the mother. She said that she was the mother's sister and told the foster parents that it was an aunt's obligation to keep looking out for her nephew.

The plot of this true tale seems like it comes from the pen of Charles Dickens so filled it is with emotional drama.

Finally, after about 2 ½ years, baby Boynton was adopted by the Carlson's. Mr. Carlson was a somewhat successful wool broker, and his nurturing wife was thrilled to provide a good home.

Unfortunately, tragedy struck again when Mr. Carlson passed away when his adopted son was only 12 years old.

Mrs. Carlson scrimped and saved and did everything she could to give her adopted only son a decent life.

The boy had ambition and wanted to make something of himself. He graduated from the Naval Academy preparatory school, seemingly destined for great things. He was admitted to the University of Mississippi using an ROTC scholarship opportunity. However, he soon grew disenchanted with college life and left the university without graduating.

The seemingly wayward Richard Carlson then moved to Los Angeles hoping to find success amidst the palm trees and beautiful weather on the West Coast. He began working as a copy boy for the *Los Angeles Times* and before you knew it, he talked himself into a job as a reporter for *United Press International*.

His friend Carl Brisson, as the son of movie star Rosalind Russell, introduced Carlson to the biggest gossip columnist in America, Louella Parsons. Parsons put her weekly column together in a posh Beverly Hills office and the fast talking Carlson convinced her to allow him to chase down stories when he wasn't working for UPI.

Parsons could see that Carlson was industrious and more importantly she identified his raw writing talent. Carlson wasn't exactly in the big time, but he was rubbing elbows with powerful people.

Carlson then began freelancing as a reporter for various television stations, forming his own independent production company creating stories for TV stations all over the country.

Carlson's writing skills surfaced in a big way when he

collaborated with his friend Carl, selling a story to *Look Magazine*. The article was a lengthy exposé connecting the Mayor of San Francisco with the Mafia. Carlson's name was now famous on a national level despite the fact that *Look Magazine* was found liable for defamation because of that article.

Carlson escaped personal liability in relation to the *Look Magazine* libel lawsuit and he decided to get serious about a career in television.

KABC-TV in Los Angeles was one of the most important television stations in America. Carlson worked jointly with TV producer Pete Noyes and Carlson achieved greater notoriety as various television awards, including a *Peabody*, began to crowd his mantle at home. Carlson was on the launchpad of an incredible career in television as Noyes brought Carlson to KFMB-TV in San Diego.

Carlson was an anchorman reading the news but was also given the freedom to create his own investigative reports. Carlson and his camera crew broke a lot of important stories in San Diego and the television world was beginning to pay attention.

He made headlines during a time when transsexualism was rarely discussed in public. Carlson produced an exposé of a transgender con-man that garnered significant national attention.

Media professionals were shocked when Carlson suddenly left the San Francisco television station, vowing never to return. Carlson had become disillusioned because he realized that television sponsors wanted him to continue to produce sex scandals instead of meaningful news stories.

In 1977, Carlson landed on his feet, becoming vice-president of a newly formed bank in San Francisco. Carlson excelled in this job but eventually found himself mired in a home foreclosure scandal that was about to become the focus of a *60 Minutes* interview conducted by the hard-boiled Mike Wallace from CBS news.

In a brilliant move that sounds like the kind of thing Tucker Carlson would do today, Richard Carlson hired his own camera crew to videotape the interview as a guard against unfair editing by the producers of *60 Minutes*. Richard Carlson's videotape crew ended up with footage of Mike Wallace telling some pretty racist jokes.

Game, set, and match. Mike Wallace and the *60 Minutes* people had to give up on their persecution of Carlson and his bank because they themselves had been found to be dirty with the mud of racism all over their hands.

At this point, you'd say that Richard Carlson had already had a pretty amazing career, but the truth is he was just getting started.

Having covered politicians for years, you'd think that Carlson would stay away from the world's dirtiest profession. You would be wrong.

In 1984, Richard Carlson, the orphanage waif, became a candidate for mayor of the City of San Diego. It turned out to be one of the most brutal municipal campaigns in history.

Carlson played dirty, implying that his opponent was linked to the gay community. Remember, in the early 80s the gay community was not an important political force. Candidates so linked often suffered at the polls.

The mud was now flying frequently and by the bucket-full in this amazing mayor's race. Carlson's opponent told audiences that Carlson was using his connections in the banking industry to squeeze campaign donations from the ultra-wealthy, which could only lead to a mayor who would forget about the little guy.

Carlson lost the race despite spending over a million dollars on the campaign. That was a lot of money to spend on a losing effort back in those days. Carlson told himself that he would never put his name on the ballot again. The experience was that brutal.

The San Diego mayoral campaign however did yield some benefit for the bereft Richard Carlson. He had been able to rub elbows with important Republican leaders throughout the country and even became friends with California Republican Governor Pete Wilson.

These contacts soon produced dividends as President Ronald Reagan nominated Carlson to serve as the Associate Director of the United States Information Agency at the behest of his friend Pete Wilson. The U.S. Information Agency was an organization funded by the United States Congress to operate Radio Free Europe and the Voice Of America.

Soon Carlson became the director of the Voice Of America and he honed the organization into a top-flight news agency that carried the message of American capitalism and democracy to foreign countries otherwise ignorant of the inspiring story of America. Carlson had found his niche.

The man who loved dynamic news reporting now had close to 3000 employees delivering news all over the world. It was an extremely professional organization that rivaled the news departments of the three major broadcast networks.

The Voice Of America was important because it broadcast news in the native tongue of countries anxious to hear about the USA. Foreign governments often attempted jamming of the radio and television signals coming from the Voice Of

America but Carlson used advanced technology to foil their efforts.

Carlson was a major news figure and he felt that he was fighting for truth on the side of the angels. He was. His Voice Of America was broadcasting 24/7 to more than 140 million people hungry for reliable authentic news from the United States.

Carlson was soon confronted with a major challenge at the Voice Of America. The agency was being pressured to reduce spending by eliminating the foreign-language specialists who were otherwise the key to international success. Carlson was spending a lot of money to make sure that they were broadcasting in 45 different languages across the globe.

But now, Carlson was directed to limit broadcasts to only four or five languages as a way to save millions of dollars.

Carlson decided to play a very dramatic hand. He assembled all of the Voice Of America employees in an auditorium where everyone was anxious to hear Carlson's pronouncements.

A hush came over the crowd as Carlson asked all the foreign-language specialists to stand. He then announced to the assemblage that all of these employees were about to be fired in order to save money even though the international reach of the Voice Of America was only made possible because of this foreign-language expenditure.

The audience was outraged and soon the story was circulating throughout the media world that cost cutters were trying to cut the heart out of the Voice Of America. Those fighting the Cold War knew that the Voice Of America was an important tool in the war against communism.

Ardent conservatives told the cost cutters to pound salt and Richard Carlson's gamble paid off. The language specialists remained in place and Richard Carlson was the man who saved the day.

Carlson's rescue of The Voice Of America did not go unnoticed and in 1991 President George Herbert Walker Bush rewarded him with an appointment as ambassador to the Seychelles, a small but important Caribbean nation.

This did not last long however, because Carlson loved media and the Voice Of America experience had made him a true believer in the power of good broadcasting. In 1992 Carlson was appointed Chief Executive Officer of the Corporation for Public Broadcasting, otherwise known as PBS.

Carlson fought hard to change the public's perception of PBS which was suffering from the conservative perception that PBS had a liberal bias. Carlson recognized that many of the PBS employees had a liberal bent, but he also saw its potential to accurately report the news without the influence of corporate sponsors who often controlled the direction of news reporting at the privately run broadcast networks.

Carlson was at PBS for five years and during that time the public network really did function with political neutrality. He wouldn't have it any other way.

Next, it was time for Richard Carlson to make some big money in the private sector. He became the president of one of the divisions of *King World*. This was a gigantic syndication company broadcasting *Oprah*, *Wheel of Fortune*, and *Jeopardy*. In 1999, CBS purchased *King World* for almost $3 billion and Carlson was now out of the media broadcast business. The huge money from CBS however, meant that he was leaving with a solid gold parachute.

He was a happy man who had spectacular career and

somehow managed to hang onto his integrity through the whole thing.

Richard Carlson, who goes by the name Dick with his friends, remains active to this very day. His son Tucker sees his father frequently and loves him dearly. Tucker has inherited the legacy of integrity in media established by this malnourished orphan who became one of the most powerful and respected names in journalism and media.

This truly is one of the instances where if you want to understand the son, you need to look at the life of the father.

Those that have interviewed Richard Carlson have noticed something about him that is also true about his son Tucker. Both Carlson's wear a rubber band on their wrist. Richard explains that the simple rubber band reminds him of his roots in journalism at *The Los Angeles Times* where he started.

In those days, newspaper advertising inserts would be bound together by a simple rubber band. Richard Carlson began wearing the rubber band to remind him to be humble and think about where he came from, never letting his ego get in the way and never letting his achievements crowd out the memory of his difficult childhood story.

Tucker's Father Richard Carlson offering advice to President Gerald Ford.

Tucker Carlson followed his lead. Richard, Tucker, and his brother Buckley wear that rubber band in order to assure themselves that they have a lot to be thankful for.

CHAPTER 8
IRAQI STORY

There are a number of events throughout Carlson's journalistic and television career that influenced his political philosophy. However, nothing impacted Carlson's view of the world more than his spending time with American forces in something our government called *Operation Iraqi Freedom* after we engineered the fall of the despotic Saddam Hussein.

Saddam was a horrible person who promoted torture and rape. He murdered his enemies and suspected enemies and even murdered their children.

What happened in Iraq initiated Carlson's hate of neocons. This word is short for neoconservative or "new" conservative. These neocons were the Republicans in the Bush administration and in both houses of Congress who were convinced that American soldiers in Iraq could plant the seeds of democracy while traveling the country armed with high-powered weapons and Humvees.

Tucker did not disagree with the neocon view that the

people of Iraq deserved liberation from the totalitarianism of Saddam.

But that's where Tucker's agreement ended.

Tucker Carlson traveled to Iraq in 2003 to become an observer of the military operators tasked with bringing American-style freedom and citizen participation in choosing government leaders.

Essentially, Carlson wanted to see how things were going in America's effort to help these downtrodden people walk gently into the light of self-determinative governance.

Almost immediately upon landing in Iraq, Carlson was confronted with the reality that every American was an enemy to be shot, stabbed, or blown up at every opportunity.

The American soldiers were constantly on edge. Wherever they went, they were resented and in the eyes of the Iraqi citizens, they deserved to die.

For this reason, the common theme throughout the trip was one of intense fear, Carlson bouncing from one crisis to another, almost getting killed on several occasions throughout the trip.

Carlson described that the sense of resentment on the part of the Iraqi people was palpable. He remembered hundreds of Iraqi citizens waiting in line at a gas station so they could get their ancient trucks and farm equipment operating in a country were very few gas stations were actually open for business. The military convoy in which Carlson was embedded interrupted the Iraqi citizens

Carlson carried a weapon in Iraq. He is smiling but was scared out of his mind.

patiently waiting their turn to get gas, the convoy commandeering the gas station, taking all fuel that it needed while the Iraqi citizens stared at them with hate.

Carlson saw this American military gas station take-over as somewhat jarring but didn't complain at the time because he also realized that waiting around for their own turn would just leave the Americans sitting ducks for snipers always on the hunt for people wearing the American flag patch.

Tucker's survival therefore depended on this American arrogance, but he couldn't help feeling that these impoverished native people deserved a little more consideration.

At one point, Carlson used a satellite phone to speak with his wife to let her know that everything was okay. Bullets began to fly in the middle of the conversation and Carlson found himself running and ducking as unseen assailants showered the compound with bullets. He told his wife that it was nothing and ended the conversation, hoping that he would be alive the next day.

The situation was so severe that Tucker himself was issued a rifle along with appropriate instructions and a bulletproof vest. Tucker, an experienced hunter, knew his way around firearms but even he didn't expect this.

Carlson realized that every non-American had to be viewed with suspicion because the anti-American sentiment was so strong and pervasive that showing any vulnerability might lead straight to a body bag.

For this reason, the American military spoke loudly and gruffly to the Iraqi citizens in all circumstances. Carlson could see the Americans were like animal trainers constantly barking commands in order to establish who's boss. The American military always spoke in condescending tones of superiority. They knew these Iraqi citizens didn't want them there, even if they had driven out the feared Saddam.

Carlson also hated the situation because it seemed that half of the operation was undertaken by contractors, private companies employing mostly men to provide logistical support for the military.

The private contractors consisted mostly of former military and former American policemen willing to travel to the Middle East because of the fabulous pay. Contract employees most of the time were paid 5 to 10 times the base salary earned by a member of the United States Marine Corps.

The worst part of the contractors was that they did not have to follow military protocol and they did not have to follow rules of engagement. Each contract employee carried his own weapons chosen by the employee because of their accessibility and their lethality.

It was like being in the old wild West. Contractors had very little respect for the lives of non-Americans. It wasn't uncommon for a contractor to shoot a couple of Iraqi citizens in the head after the contractor claimed the citizen looked like he was reaching for a gun. Iraq was a very scary place and a very sad place at this time.

Carlson recounted a time when three young men in their 20s were seen milling about near the American outpost. The Americans essentially engaged in a form of stop and frisk of these three Iraqi men. Accompanying the American military was another man who was a foreign mercenary working for Uncle Sam for big bucks. He asked the American lieutenant in charge of our patrol if he could shoot the three young men.

None of the three posed any kind of threat as they were unarmed. They did however seem to have a heightened resentment of the American presence and a smart-alecky attitude.

Carlson was reminded of the smart-ass approach POW John McCain had shown to his captors.

The Lieutenant turned to the mercenary and told him not to shoot the three men. The mercenary was disappointed.

Tucker realized that if the Lieutenant had given the green light, three young lives would've been snuffed out instantly. Carlson comprehended that this scene was likely being replicated all throughout the country except that the shooting of the innocent was probably frequently given the green light.

Carlson was seeing firsthand the arrogant self-righteousness of the neocons back in Washington. The Washington intelligentsia were convinced that they could force-feed democracy to Iraqi citizens at the end of a gun barrel.

The presumptuousness of these fools sending American soldiers into unbelievable danger, thinking they could overcome thousands of years of Islamic culture!

Worse still was that the neocons thought that American firepower could overcome the basic principle of human nature that says that nobody wants to be taken over by an occupying force.

And in Iraq, we were definitely an occupying force. Unwelcome and unwanted.

Iraqi citizens felt that Americans viewed themselves as entitled to take over the country because Saddam the dictator had been removed under the overwhelming force of the American flag.

The Washington idiot decision-makers thought the Americans would be welcomed just like General Patton when he liberated Paris from Nazi control.

The highly educated eggheads in the Bush administration thought it was just a simple matter of teaching the Iraqis about constitutional rights and setting up voter registration as a prerequisite to free elections.

Carlson saw that the entire project was a disaster, and he even expressed some feelings of guilt because he had previously cheered George W. Bush and his philosophy of "nation building".

Carlson's presence in Iraq changed his thinking. The military-industrial complex President Eisenhower had warned us all about was in fact profiting by the billions to support a fantasy plan that was never going to work.

What really galled Carlson was that Americans were being killed and Iraqi families and even Iraqi children were dying, expendable in an environment where the philosophy was either kill or be killed.

Tucker worried about the loss of the American soul. Military operations attempted to snuff out pockets of Iraqi resistance even if the innocent were sadly categorized as collateral damage.

Carlson knew that this evil the-end-justifies-the-means philosophy in Iraq was especially disturbing because the end was impossible to achieve anyhow. The American military and its thousands of private contractor assistants would never be able to overcome cultural barriers to install an American-style form of government.

Something inside Tucker Carlson was indeed killed in Iraq. Carlson's faith in American leadership was gone. The neocons had completely bamboozled the American people and the world.

At one point Carlson even wrote that his Iraqi experience

convinced him that neocons were merely "liberals with guns".

Of course Carlson was right about all of this and he pledged never to be fooled again. He promised that if given the opportunity, he would use whatever platform he was given to pull away the mask of fake conservatism masquerading as patriotism.

Tucker Carlson was and truly is an American patriot. But going forward, he would have a clearer vision.

Carlson was able to make it back to the USA in one piece but now he was changed forever, and he was ready to tell the world all about it.

CHAPTER 9

FRAUDS

Another feature of the Tucker Carlson personality is that he hates frauds.

And whatever the platform Tucker stands on, whether it be an obscure column in a little-known periodical, or before the cameras on cable TV that carry his words clear across the globe, Tucker Carlson is a heatseeking missile hell-bent on the destruction of frauds.

He makes no secret of it, and you cannot help cheering him on when he goes on one of his crusades against an obvious charlatan.

There are few things more spectacular to watch than a Tucker Carlson takedown on national television.

Toward the end of his tenure at Fox News, it became almost impossible to book guests willing to stand in opposition to Tucker Carlson.

Word had spread throughout the media world that opposing Tucker on camera was the equivalent of allowing yourself to undergo an autopsy at the city morgue while you were still living.

Opposing Tucker on camera was painful and occasionally could even lead to the end of your career.

It got to the point where left-wing thinkers concluded that you are damned if you do and damned if you don't.

If you did appear against Tucker, you would be destroyed by his interruptions and bulldog determination to force you to answer questions that you prefer to deflect. You would also be criticized for even making an appearance on Tucker Carlson because some on the left viewed appearing for a Tucker interview as inadvertently lending credibility to Carlson and to Fox News. Some on the left even viewed appearing on the Tucker program as an act of treason no matter how much of a fight you put up during the interview.

You are damned if you don't appear with Tucker because you then allow him to misrepresent your position instead of getting the unfiltered opposing viewpoint straight from the horse's mouth.

And the Tucker Carlson takedowns are indeed legendary. You have to do a lot of hunting on the Internet because *YouTube* and *Google* like to diminish the search rankings for Carlson since they essentially hate him and want to reduce your access to his programming.

But if you are creative, you can find scores of piping hot interviews where Tucker Carlson slices and dices those who pretend to be noble and righteous.

Here are a few examples.

On March 21, 2017, Baltimore City Councilman Zeke Cohen entered into the lion's den of a Tucker Carlson interview. Cohen knew what the interview was about and he had ample opportunity to prepare himself to do battle with the Fox News host. Even with that foreknowledge, Carlson nuked him on national television.

Despite the fact that an illegal immigrant had recently raped a 14-year-old girl in a Baltimore school, Councilman Cohen introduced legislation to prohibit immigration law enforcement in the City of Baltimore. Tucker Carlson criticized the proposed ordinance because the rape could've been prevented if the 18-year-old perpetrator had been deported before it could occur. The Councilman doubled down on his proposal, feeling the new law was necessary because he felt that immigration officials were too much like Nazi brownshirts.

But Carlson would not let go of his original view: prohibiting immigration enforcement could possibly lead to further tragedies like the rape of this young girl. Carlson looked at the Councilman with contempt, raising his voice as he accused the municipal legislator of opening the door to the occurrence of further tragedy and violence.

The councilman was ill-equipped to deal with the onslaught from Carlson. He nervously kept checking his notes hoping to find some golden phrase that could rescue him from the Carlson attack. In the end, he seemed to give up, his face with that blank look that admitted to the nation "I got nothing."

Carlson then cut to a commercial, the devastated remains of Councilman Cohen alone in the Baltimore studio where he had been the victim of another Tucker Carlson execution conducted by remote camera.

For Carlson however, it was just another takedown of a fraud posing as someone interested in doing good things. Another classic Tucker Carlson dissection of a human being live on camera involved Lisa Durden.

Professor Durden was a teacher of political science at Essex College when she came on the Tucker show to defend a

Black Lives Matter program in which white people were specifically prohibited from attending. The *BLM* program in question was designed to celebrate Memorial Day but only from the perspective of black soldiers who had given their lives. Carlson had no problem with the project designed to honor African American soldiers who had made the ultimate sacrifice to protect our country.

His problem was with the *BLM* organizers sponsoring the Memorial Day activity. The sponsors indicated in writing that white people were not welcome to attend the event. Carlson railed against the racist segregation message conveyed by this "no whites allowed" policy. Professor Durden appeared on the program as a major *BLM* supporter and participant defending the prohibition of white skinned individuals.

Carlson was in rare form that night and demonstrated that the principles of racial equality and colorblindness established by the Reverend Doctor Martin Luther King were being trampled on by *Black Lives Matter* in this case. Professor Durden sarcastically mocked Carlson as a wounded oppressor who was finally getting a little bit of his own racial supremacy medicine.

This really set Carlson off as he castigated Durden for her adherence to concepts of segregation that heretofore had been long opposed by American civil rights leaders. Carlson successfully painted her as a hypocrite trying to divide people instead of promoting the unity fair-minded Americans have been striving for. The interview ended with the professor throwing epithets at the host as an alternative to logical arguments. She was defeated and BLM really took it on the chin in the eyes of most Americans because of this interview.

The real point is this: Tucker Carlson does not suffer fools and if you try to pull the wool over his eyes, especially on television, he will figuratively cut you like a stuffed pig. Challenging him on camera is always a bad idea because Carlson always does his research and he can call upon the data in a microsecond. He rarely has to look at his notes when he goes into debate mode because his steel trap mind has all the information at the ready like weapons prepared to dispatch the enemy.

Tucker's opposition to frauds and fakes actually goes back a long way.

Carlson's exposing of the hypocrisy of former South Carolina Senator Ernest Hollings is the stuff legends are made of. In his book *Politicians, Partisans, and Parasites*, Carlson spends several pages talking about the racist Senator asking for the black vote in the heart of the deep South in South Carolina.

What Carlson hated the most about Hollings was that he would describe himself as a sensitive Democratic leader concerned about the civil rights of his black constituents while simultaneously issuing forth with the kind of racial invectives that would be more typical of a Klansman than of a modern statesman.

Carlson pointed out that Hollings referred to Jewish Senator Howard Metzenbaum of Ohio as "the senator from B'nai B'rith". Carlson wanted to make sure everybody knew about this racist remark even though Hollings was able to successfully have the statement obliterated from the Congressional record.

Carlson attacked Senator Hollings because of his racist views of leadership from African nations. Hollings told his friends that African leaders attended international conferences so that they could enjoy normal meals instead of eating each other back in their home countries. Hollings thought of presidents from African nations as merely cannibals on vacation.

Carlson admitted that Hollings was a great television guest but that was just because he was such a caricature of southern good old boy politics managing to flimflam minority voters into supporting him because he ran under the banner of the Democratic Party supposedly looking out for opportunities for black citizens. Carlson compared Hollings' pronouncements to those of the famous Foghorn Leghorn from Looney Tunes cartoons.

The comparison was spot on. Carlson wanted everyone to know that Senator Hollings was actually a hypocritical blowhard enjoying the trappings of public office without actually caring about the future of his constituents.

If you get the chance, find a copy of the Carlson book with the section on Senator Hollings. It is great writing with a lot of wit and sharp commentary.

Carlson throughout his career also spent a fair amount of time exposing two frauds that nonetheless created very successful careers.

These two men are Jesse Jackson and Al Sharpton. He calls both of these men "race hustlers".

He has written through the years about the way that Jesse Jackson morphed from an apprentice civil rights leader who learned at the side of the great Martin Luther King into a shakedown artist.

Jesse Jackson indeed worked along Dr. King on many projects of *Southern Christian Leadership Conference* (SCLC). The SCLC was the banner organization behind civil rights projects in Selma and Montgomery and the huge confluence of citizens at the foot of the Lincoln Memorial where Dr. King delivered his famous I have a dream speech.

After Dr. King was assassinated, it seemed that Ralph Abernathy, the number two man in the SCLC, would assume the mantle of leadership worn for so long by MLK. However, it was Jesse Jackson who emerged from those dark days after the assassination as the new spokesman for civil rights to whom national media and reporters turned for commentary on the American situation. Jesse Jackson was a much better public speaker than Abernathy and he projected a real magnetism as a dramatic preacher in the mold of Dr. King. In fact, the Jackson style was more flamboyant than Dr. King and soon he was identified as the most prominent moral voice preaching equality and brotherhood.

Carlson saw Jackson's preaching as electric but his ethics lacking.

What Carlson despised about Jackson was the way he used his position of moral leadership to extract finances from rich white people as way to absolve them of their guilty past. Jackson formed something called the Rainbow Coalition and Operation Push headquartered in Chicago. Both organizations were converted by Jackson into a form of black mafia telling corporate America to pay protection money to Jackson to insulate corporations from Jackson's attacks on racist corporate hiring policies and racist business practices.

Everyone in America knew that our biggest corporations maintained a white hierarchy catering to the white consumer while millions of black Americans barely scraped by in squalid black ghettos in the inner cities of our country's great metropolises. Carlson realized that Jackson wasn't looking for solution. He was looking for a payday. A big payday.

Carlson observed the growth of Jackson's personal wealth and the expansion of his penetration into the media world while poor black Americans couldn't seem to escape the repeating cycle of welfare and the disintegration of the black family.

For these reasons Carlson did not like Jesse Jackson and frequently issued commentary or wrote columns to that effect.

At one point, one of the cable networks gave Jesse Jackson his own TV show and Carlson made an appearance as he was becoming more well-known in the talking head circuit. Carlson found Jackson to be uninformed and unable to speak intelligently even regarding civil rights issues without resorting to issuing forth with one of his stock clichés. Carlson realized that Jesse Jackson wasn't so much a leader as a hollowed-out pretender to the throne that had been built by the great Martin Luther King.

Although at one point Jesse Jackson sought the Democratic nomination for president, Jackson eventually faded into obscurity leaving in his wake only his trade slogan "keep hope alive".

The other race hustler fraud that has been identified by Carlson over the years is Al Sharpton.

Carlson demonstrated a much higher level of respect for Sharpton in comparison to Jesse Jackson. As Jesse Jackson faded into history, Al Sharpton stepped up as the new leader of the civil rights movement in the USA.

Part of Carlson's respect for Sharpton in contrast to Jesse

Jackson arose from the fact that Sharpton seemed to have authentic credentials and skills as a Christian preacher. Carlson wrote about the time he observed Sharpton preach for over an hour making specific accurate references to sections of the Bible. Sharpton knew the Old and New Testament from beginning to end and used that knowledge to punctuate his dynamic sermons throughout his career.

Carlson was especially impressed by the fact that Sharpton could speak extemporaneously for a long time without notes. In fact, Carlson observed, Sharpton always spoke without the benefit of a prepared text or even notes and every time his biblical references were outstandingly accurate. So to some extent Carlson admired Sharpton as a man of real talent and ability.

What he didn't like was that Sharpton sought notoriety and fame by ratcheting up racial tensions and division through lies and fabrication.

The Tawana Brawley case in 1987 is one of the standout examples of Al Sharpton's willingness to sell his soul to the devil just to enhance his public profile. In that case, a young teenage black girl ran away from home but afraid to face the wrath of her father, she made up a story about being raped by six white men. The father of course pushed for an investigation of the alleged crime and Al Sharpton essentially took over the situation making several incendiary statements about white people on local and national television. Sharpton was now officially a celebrity.

The case went before a jury who unanimously determined that the entire crime was a hoax created by young girl who just wanted an alibi to present to her father because of her disappearance.

After the jury proved the untruthfulness of the tale,

Sharpton doubled down and even said that the prosecuting attorney was himself personally one of the six rapists. Sharpton knew no shame when it came to tall tales and this even increased his celebrity further.

Just a few years later it was clear that there was no place in the country where the existence of racial tensions couldn't be increased by the presence of Reverend Al Sharpton. It seems that Sharpton fashioned himself a professional racial antagonist. In the Crown Heights case, a Jewish tenant threatened to evict his black subtenant in a small storefront in New York City. The Jewish man doing the evicting was himself a tenant because the building was owned by a black Pentecostal church. This didn't matter to Sharpton.

Sharpton sought out every reporter and media correspondent he could find to attack the attempted eviction as the epitome of white Jews trying to control the fate of black people. Racial animus was inflamed by Sharpton's rhetoric and the result was tragic.

One of the protesters stirred up by Sharpton entered the storefront and shot dead every white person he could find shouting "we're going to see that this cracker suffers."

Seven white customers were killed by the black protester who merely saw himself as a human sword of justice working under the direction of the noble Reverend Al Sharpton.

Carlson saw Sharpton as the ultimate outside agitator ready to helicopter in to every situation where he might be able to burnish his image as America's number one moral leader on the issue of racial justice.

In a weird way, Carlson sort of admired Al Sharpton because he was very good at manufacturing publicity. It's just that Carlson could not stomach that he was willing to lie regardless of who got hurt or in some cases regardless of who got shot.

As Carlson's media career expanded, he crossed paths with Al Sharpton on numerous occasions. Carlson realized that Sharpton might've been a race hustler, but Sharpton kept himself well-informed and really was articulate when it came to debating civil rights issues. Carlson noticed that Sharpton continued shaking down corporate leadership similar to his predecessor, but that Sharpton, at least as a media personality, pursued substantive arguments and data to back up his positions.

Carlson did not like frauds and for this reason did not like Al Sharpton. However, Carlson was willing to give the devil his due. Sharpton played the media game well and educated himself to make sure that he would be a worthy opponent on the debate stage.

In 2004, Al Sharpton ran for president and Carlson was impressed by the way he calmly waited his turn to say his peace debating with all the other candidates.

Despite that, Carlson still hates frauds and looks for every opportunity to shoot them down like a surface to air missile.

Lest you think that the famous Tucker Carlson destruction of frauds act is limited to his attacks on Democrats, I must point you to one of the better Carlson takedowns that occurred not that long ago on the Fox News Channel.

As the war in Ukraine escalated, Carlson's criticism of America's unlimited spending to provide the Ukrainians with weapons escalated as well. Tucker Carlson coherently explained that his opposition was twofold. First of all, America's financial strength was being diminished through this unlimited bleeding of American resources. To him, it seemed that the Biden administration and both houses of

Congress were willing to spend any amount necessary to help President Zelinski of Ukraine defeat Vladimir Putin and the Russians.

Secondly, and perhaps more importantly according to Carlson, participating in this proxy war against Putin would bring America perilously close to the possibility of a nuclear conflagration with the Soviet leader. Carlson was exasperated that American leaders were willing to risk armageddon in defense of the country with whom we have little in common and whose defense did not seem to be of particular importance to the United States. In other words, we were spending money that we didn't have on a cause that could lead to our own destruction.

Enter Congresswoman Maria Salazar from Florida. Fox News played a video of her comments that she was willing to spend any amount of money as would be necessary and would be willing to take virtually any action needed in order to defeat Putin's progress in the Ukraine.

Carlson reviewed the tape and genuinely believed that the Congresswoman was behaving foolishly as were all her colleagues in Congress.

So he invited the Congresswoman to appear on the Tucker Carlson show for a brief repartee with Tucker Carlson himself.

This is a pretty interesting situation because Maria Salazar was viewed as one of the up-and-coming progressive Republicans in the United States House of Representatives. A former news reporter herself, she was known as a good debater who could hold her own against the very best. She was smart and well-informed and known for the fact that she wouldn't take any crap from anybody. Including Tucker Carlson.

Salazar agreed to the appearance.

Big mistake.

Carlson saw the appearance as an opportunity to shoot holes in another neocon-inspired effort from the military-industrial complex. The neocons convinced legislators as well as the President of the United States and everyone in the State and Defense Departments that morality demanded our full support of Ukraine.

Carlson was ready.

Through the first half of the exchange the Congresswoman continued to push back against Carlson's desire to limit America's unlimited spending for Ukrainian weaponry. But the Congresswoman fell flat on her face in responding to Carlson's arguments that our expanded Ukrainian involvement could result in a nuclear response from Putin.

She just could not produce a coherent answer when faced with the argument that tweaking Putin's nose could easily end in the destruction of the entire planet.

But it was Tucker Carlson's mastery of facts that led to Salazar's being pronounced dead on arrival in the media morgue. Carlson asked the Congresswoman, who is a member of the foreign affairs committee of the United States Congress, how many nuclear weapons were at the disposal of Vladimir Putin.

She stumbled for a moment and admitted that she did not know the number. Carlson looked her dead in the eye and told her that Putin had access to 6000 nukes.

There was a pause in the discussion. She was toast. Stick a fork in her. Carlson even commented that he was surprised that a person so willing to give Ukrainians military help was unfamiliar with the extent of the Russian nuclear arsenal.

Carlson made her look stupid and unprepared and although the discussion continued, it was clear that Carter Carlson was standing on the winner's podium.

As I said, Carlson does not like frauds and if you take an important position, you'd better have the facts to support your position and if you don't, you will be revealed by Carlson to be a fraud.

As Carlson closed out the interview with Salazar, he thanked her for coming on because, he told her, it was becoming very difficult to get opponents to come on to the program against Tucker.

No kidding.

Like I said at the beginning of this chapter, Tucker Carlson is a heatseeking missile looking for targets in the form of frauds and posers.

This is just one of the things that makes him great.

CHAPTER 10
LOVES TO LAUGH

A nother endearing quality that has created legions of loyal fans for Tucker Carlson is the fact that he loves to laugh and doesn't mind doing it on camera.

This was a real contrast in comparison to Tucker's predecessor, Bill O'Reilly, who owned the 8 o'clock hour and cable news for many years while he hosted a program called *The O'Reilly Factor*. It was not uncommon for O'Reilly to become hot and agitated with anger directed at a guest who was obviously lying.

O'Reilly was always yelling during his program and viewers loved watching it as O'Reilly dispatched his opponent who took on the character of a cornered animal.

While O'Reilly certainly smiled throughout his programs, you almost never caught him laughing on air. O'Reilly pictured himself as too much of a serious newsman attacking deceivers. It would simply be beneath him to let loose with guffaws and giggles during his important highly rated program.

Tucker Carlson, by contrast, was more comfortable with himself and he felt free to express his emotions right on camera as they bubbled up to the surface in front of millions of viewers. All of us have had a moment where we are put off by someone who thinks they are so funny that they laugh at their own jokes.

Somehow, Tucker Carlson was able to get away with it. During his opening monologues, he would describe an opponent's idiocies punctuated by his quick repeating tenor laugh that threatened to escalate into some of the soprano range of his voice.

Genuine absurdities coming from the mouth of someone like Alexandria Ocasio-Cortez or Pete Buttigieg would send Tucker Carlson into gales of high pitched laughter, Carlson rocking forward and backward as he did so. Sometimes Carlson laughed so hard that you almost felt that he was coming close to falling off his chair.

The secret to Carlson's success here was that the thing that made him laugh indeed was so absurd that you had to laugh with him. America was rolling in the aisles as Tucker Carlson described moronic practices of left-wing dunderheads.

If the laughter were forced or faked it would never have worked. But Carlson could begin a very serious and somber toned monologue only to practically bust a gut laughing at stupidities generated by left-leaning pundits from other networks or President Biden's press secretary.

In fact, at universities all across America, a new drinking game emerged among conservative Republican undergraduates.

The college students would gather around the television screen during Tucker Carlson's weeknight monologues. You had to drink 3 ounces of beer every time Tucker laughed during the monologue. Some nights were pretty easy but on other nights when Tucker was really enjoying himself college kids would be completely wasted by the time Carlson finished his monologue around 8:20 PM Eastern Standard Time.

The truth is Tucker's laugh is infectious because it's so darn authentic. You listen to his presentation and start laughing together the way you do with a good friend sharing a laugh together the way only good friends can. Tucker Carlson may have been a conservative pundit but for millions of Americans he was a buddy, the two of you having a great time at the expense of some left-wing moron.

Carlson's laughter, it turns out, is actually one of his calling cards when it comes to his broadcast personality.

Carlson tells the story of a nutty congressman from Youngstown, Ohio by the name of Jim Traficant. He appeared on Carlson's talk show completely drunk and hitting on various female assistant producers. But what really made Carlson laugh was the vision of Traficant's weird hairdo that resembled a dead squirrel glued to the top of his head. If I had to seriously interrogate someone with a squirrel head, I would laugh also.

The urge to laugh almost got Tucker into some real trouble on one occasion. One of Tucker's favorite guests back in the old days was a retired District of Columbia homicide detective, Ted Williams. Williams still pops up as a guest on Fox news on some of their current programming. Sean Hannity uses him as an expert on a regular basis.

In any case, Carlson was interviewing Williams related to a very serious story involving a woman murdered at a *Home*

Depot store. Former Detective Williams wanted Carlson to know that this murder was especially tragic because the victim had recently successfully fought a battle with breast cancer.

Unfortunately, the detective said it was an especially tragic event *because the victim had recently received breast implants.*

Tucker was seized with an uncontrollable urge to explode with laughter over the detective's verbal mistake. The idea that a hard-boiled police expert was saddened by the shooting death of a lady because she recently had a boob job was too much.

Former DC Detective Ted Williams activated Carlson's funny bone in the middle of an interview.

It usually happens on local news broadcasts where one of the anchors or the weatherman mispronounce a word creating a *double entendre.* The laughter builds instantaneously like a pressure cooker with steam that must be vented.

The Ted Williams story tells you everything you need to know about Tucker Carlson and his laughter. Tucker's laughter helps us relate to him as a person. All of us like to laugh and when the joke is a good one, we want to enjoy having someone laugh with us.

Of all the many tools in Tucker Carlson's television broadcast arsenal, his laughter is one tool his competitors just don't have. And that is part of what makes Tucker Carlson special.

CHAPTER 11
TRUTH TO POWER

The planet Earth has three essential levels from the standpoint of geology. The outer level has the crust where we find clay, sand, rocks, soil, and of course, bodies of water. Deep inside the center of the earth you find the solid core which has been unchangeable over millions and perhaps billions of years. But the middle level between the crust and the core is where you find unbelievably hot liquefied metals swirling and flowing in erratic and random patterns.

This metallic steaming pudding outside the core but beneath the crust affects the magnetic polarity of the earth on a regular basis. Approximately 800,000 years ago this metallic concoction moved in such a way as to reverse the earth's polarity to its present state. In other words, the north and south poles switched polarity to the present-day condition so that your compass points to the north. Prior to that switch, your compass would've pointed to the south.

It is unbelievable to think that such a major geologic factor such as polarity could completely reverse itself. Scientists studying the geologic record have determined that this polarity switch has occurred several times since the origin of our planet without damage to the life systems of our world.

Despite this, the polarity shift that occurred long ago was a significantly dramatic event. Thousands of nonbiological events are impacted by the earth's magnetic polarity, ranging from the centrifugal direction of hurricanes and tornadoes to the navigational tools used by men and even animals to find their way in the world. The earth's polarity is a central operational element in the application of scientific principles.

In terms of real political and social power, the earth has undergone a complete polarity switch. What was north is now south and what was south is now north. Up is down and down is up.

We as a world and America as a nation have undergone a complete polarity switch in the last few years.

The power over all of our institutions firmly in the grasp of traditional Judeo-Christian practitioners has now been completely ceded to left-wing ideologues aggressively seeking destruction of the belief system formerly in place for many generations.

So when you hear someone from the left claiming that they are speaking truth to power, they are lying. The left now has the power and the only people speaking truth to power are those that are challenging the left.

In fact, the left's use of power is much more pervasive and aggressive than it ever was when traditionalists ruled the planet.

Years ago, traditional *liberals* fought valiantly if not to adopt left-wing concepts, at least to protect their existence in the name of the principles of free speech and free expression as found in the First Amendment to the United States Constitution.

Liberal institutions such as the American Civil Liberties Union regularly litigated so that the most unpopular ideas could be heard without suppression. In 1968, the ACLU won the right for modern-day Nazis to march in a parade in a little town called Skokie, Illinois. This community was known as a haven for survivors of Hitler's horrible holocaust. Despite this, the ACLU told the world that the First Amendment protected even the most vile theories and even the most disgusting speech.

The ACLU and institutions like this were speaking Truth To Power. They were people on the left standing up for free speech.

But with this polarity switch in control of our influential entities, all the power is on the left and truth to power means standing up to leftist power systems who want to squash those who speak the truth like a bug under your shoe.

What are those power systems?

They are corporate America, the media, the administrative state, and education.

These have always been the power centers for our nation and for the first 180 years of our existence, these power centers have been a bulwark of the national values of patriotism, faith, and family. This bulwark stood reasonably firm during the cultural changes that swept over our nation in the late 1950s and then even into the early 1990s.

Elvis, the Beatles, and Haight-Ashberry introduced the countercultural revolution that challenged our rocks of Gibraltar such as freedom, Judeo-Christian principles, and preservation of the nuclear family.

So when Abbie Hoffman and the Chicago Seven tried to disrupt the 1968 Democratic convention, Hoffman claimed that he wanted to dismantle these traditional American ideals.

These ideals were the power and he was speaking his truth to that power.

The world was shocked when tennis player Renée Richards a.k.a. Richard Raskin took aim at the power. Richards began wearing women's clothing and underwent sex reassignment surgery in the 1970s, even competing on the women's tennis circuit way back then.

The former Richard Raskin adopted the name Renée Richards and was the center of controversy for this dramatic alteration of his sex personality. Despite this, the ironclad traditional values remained dominant in America with roots running deep like giant Sequoias in the petrified Forest.

While protesters burned the American flag to show outrage over American military aggression, the average American citizen still loved the old values. An inspiring film about the dogged determination of World War II General George Patton set box office records in the 1970's. Patriotism, faith, and family were still the power and they held sway in media, corporate America, universities, and in the halls of government.

But today the power lies in the opposite hands from those years ago.

The folks that saw religion as worthless, patriotism as childish, and marital fidelity as an ancient anachronism were now in charge.

The SDS members who burned Vietnam era ROTC buildings were now taking their place in society.

They are moving into corporate board rooms, into college president offices, and into positions such as movie studio heads, news directors, and as agency heads in the federal government. Without a shot fired, power shifted from traditionalists to radicals.

In fact, you can't even call them radical anymore because they now control the mainstream.

It seems that it began to occur almost imperceptibly over the last 40 years or so, but the transition was speeding up sometime around 2010 or so. In 2010, President Obama's Affordable Care Act was passed by the United States Congress, spurred on by the left-leaning zealots who had taken over key roles in the unelected government bureaucracy.

The pace quickened. In 2015, a hit movie emerged based on a surprise bestseller "FIFTY SHADES OF GREY". The plot glorified sexual pleasure and weird pain-imposing dominatrix techniques, the idea of monogamous love in the context of the nuclear family now made irrelevant.

By the year 2016 the transition was complete. All our major institutions were marching lockstep in line with leftist ideals. Universities were now mere shells of their former selves. Free speech at a college campus, once the battle cry at Berkeley in the 1960s, was now prohibited if the speech content was traditional or conservative.

In 2017, conservative pundit and author Ann Coulter's speech at UC Berkeley was canceled by the University President who expressed security concerns. All over our nation, universities clamped down on free expression if the expression came from conservative camps.

Jordan Peterson, Ben Shapiro, Michael Knowles, scientist Tim Hunt, Matt Walsh, Dennis Prager, and more than 100 more conservative thinkers and authors have been ignominiously tossed off campuses or had their speeches cancelled because they were challenging left-wing power.

Perhaps nothing demonstrates more clearly that power has shifted from the right to the left than the example of Google's James Damore. Mr. Damore wrote an internal memo while serving as a Google engineer. He wrote that there may be factors unrelated to discrimination that cause lower women participation in engineering and stem fields.

In his memorandum, Danmore urges the hiring of more women at Google in the technology sector.

Damore merely asked if there were other influences, such as personal choice, desire to raise children, or even having an affinity for social sciences above technical sciences.

Damore merely speculated as to the relevance of these influences when women made career decisions.

He didn't criticize women's choices, but merely tried to identify what might affect those choices. Damore even offered suggestions to Google on specific ways to increase female involvement in Google technology jobs.

The media branded the memo as an anti-diversity screed and our left-wing pundits approved Google's ejecting Damore from employment.

Here's the reason this is important.

Google is by far the most influential and powerful corporation on earth. They control all your information and they have corporate wealth that would make John D. Rockefeller blush. They are the power now.

Damore tried to speak truth to power but let it be clear, the power is now all on the left.

One more example really drives home the point here.

NCAA swimming champion Riley Gaines was also an Olympic qualifier at the University of Kentucky. When she complained about competing against Leah Thomas, a transgender woman who one year prior was a less than average competitor in men's swimming, she was silenced.

The trans movement now was the power in a country that used to seek to protect the integrity of women's sports.

Worse, Gaines was attacked for criticizing that she had to dress in the same locker room with Leah Thomas who exposed his male genitals in front of the other girl swimmers in the locker room.

Exposing male organs to young girls in a female locker room not that long ago was a crime.

Today it's a noble fight for justice in this new era where the left is the power.

Because Gaines won't give up her viewpoint, she has become a flashpoint as the new power structure seeks to destroy her rather than tolerate the existence of her opinion.

Her recent speech at the University of San Francisco concluded with her being assaulted by trans activists and made prisoner in a university classroom until she could be safely escorted off campus to

Riley Gaines speaking truth to power in defense of women's sports.

freedom. The university approved the attack on Gaines.

The left has been fully installed on the seat of power.

So when you hear left-wing ideologues describing their pronouncements as speaking truth to power, you can laugh at the absurdity of it all.

Because the left has all of the power, speaking truth to

power is a reference to conservatives standing up against the left's seizure of all of our great institutions.

And when it comes to the news media, one of the leading lights in truly speaking truth to power is America's truth warrior, Tucker Carlson.

CHAPTER 12
MR. EXCITEMENT

If there is one thing that people overlook most about Tucker Carlson, it's the talent that is the heartbeat of his life.

Tucker Carlson may be known most widely for his broadcasting but at his core he is a writer.

A very good writer.

That's how he got his start in the real world of finding one's vocation.

He started writing at a small newspaper in the middle of nowhere churning out obituaries, classified advertising, and the occasional editorial.

As he climbed from one rung on the ladder to the next in the writing world, he was eventually pegged to appear on television as rising writers tended to do in the universe of cable TV, where news channels desperately sought talking heads who were coherent.

That is a low bar but Tucker was more than merely coherent. He was downright articulate and had an impressive writer's resume for such a young man.

He eventually landed the biggest of gigs at Fox News in the 8 o'clock prime time slot vacated by the dethroned O'Reilly.

But Carlson never left his original love.

Writing.

You can see this especially in the opening monologues of his broadcasts.

His writing is a blend of research, reporting, editorializing, and speculating.

Close your eyes and just listen to the opening. It's well-written prose.

It's good writing.

Frequently the key to good writing however begins with an exciting topic. This gets the juices flowing and Carlson knows it.

That's why his monologues attract such viewership. Tucker Carlson seeks out exciting stories, writes them with adrenaline flowing through his veins, and then delivers them almost breathlessly on camera, sharing his excitement with the viewer in his punchy style.

You can't help but be drawn into the story, filled with the stimulation that jumps out at you from the TV screen.

This smart guy is excited to tell you an amazing story you can't resist. It's TV electricity generated by the host.

Tucker is your brilliant next-door neighbor who meets with you in the backyard or back driveway to tell you an incredible story that no one else can tell you. And that no one else is willing to tell you.

If Carlson didn't authentically feel excited about his story, he would be a failure. But the enthusiasm he brings to the story is real, palpable.

So palpable and so exciting that millions of viewers would

build their weekday evenings around Tucker, just as they scheduled their lives around *I Love Lucy* in the late 1950s.

Americans all over the country shared their morning coffee break with friends and coworkers to discuss the previous night's disclosures on Tucker Carlson.

It was a ritual in the USA.

And the key is the excitement factor. Tucker Carlson has the writer's eye for excitement, which is just another way of saying that he can sniff out a great story when it appears on his radar.

Tucker succeeds in great part because he gets excited and chases after a great story.

This chapter is about a perfect example of how Carlson finds and pursues the exciting narrative. This is the amazing story of Tucker Carlson and his adventures with Al Sharpton.

Yes, you read that right, Al Sharpton.

Here's what happened. Back in 2003, the part-time preacher part-time civil rights activist had an idea.

To bolster his international profile and even perhaps to do some something good, Sharpton planned a trip to Liberia where he hoped to mediate peace between warring factions in the southwestern African nation.

To do this however, Sharpton had to assemble an entourage.

It was a substantial one that included Princeton's Dr. Cornell West, Archbishop Franzo King from the St. John Coltrane African Orthodox Church, and a few lieutenants of Louis J. Farrakhan's Nation of Islam.

Carlson accepted Sharpton's invitation to serve as the embedded correspondent on behalf of the American press. Carlson was actually on assignment from *Esquire Magazine.*

Carlson had worked with Sharpton on other projects and he loved Sharpton's freewheeling no hidden agenda style.

The truth was that Carlson had signed on to a daring mission. Liberian politics almost always featured bloodshed and retribution. Power changes hands at the end of machete, with the loser usually cut into pieces and fed to the pigeons.

Carlson knew the danger and the potential craziness of Sharpton's antics but he also realized that this could be the story of a lifetime.

And it was too exciting for him to miss.

The *Ghana Airways* jet made a stop off at the Azores for refueling and then headed to Ghana where Sharpton's junket would get organized and then fly in to Liberia the next day.

The game plan was to use the hotel in Ghana as a staging area before landing in Liberia the following day to meet with representatives of the opposing forces.

Sharpton was continually on his phone, confirming meetings and appointments for the next day as part of this peace mission. The stage was now set for a history making effort by Sharpton and all of those in Sharpton's posse anticipated with excitement what fruits of peace could be harvested the next day.

With the dawn came news that almost wiped out Sharpton's chances before they left. With the Liberian airport set up as the center for the negotiations, our nervous pilot plunged a dagger into Sharpton's plans, refusing to put our plane down at the Liberian airport.

The pilot was in receipt of reports of heavy artillery fighting right on the airport runways. The pilot believed our little band of peacemakers would be blown to bits maybe even as we landed or taxied to our gate. The pilot refused to keep his commitment to land at the Liberian airport.

This likely was a smart decision as Tucker and company may have been reduced to rubble.

Unfortunately, this meant that his little expedition was stranded at the less than luxurious hotel in a city called Accra in Ghana.

Tucker soon realized that the Reverend Al Sharpton was not to be denied. If he could not go to Liberia to meet with the various representatives in the conflict, he would convince them to come to him.

It worked. Before you knew it, various rooms in the hotel were occupied by the leaders of the two major factions and by the representative of the current President, Charles Taylor. Al Sharpton had the international gravitas to actually get these three groups to travel to our hotel in Ghana.

The war raging in nearby Liberia was essentially a three-part war. The reigning dictator Charles Taylor had lost enough support in the military such that he was being deposed in favor of two rival organizations both of which sought to take control of the government. It was a foregone conclusion that Taylor would soon be gone and that the country would be controlled by one of these two rival political groups.

You can imagine the chaos that reigned in Liberia as Taylor's supporters folded up their tents while the remaining two groups tried to kill each other in an effort to assume the presidency and take over the country.

A lot of blood was being shed as Taylor's last few supporters tried to stall both factions who themselves were distracted in an effort to keep the other faction from assuming power. It was a race to the bitter end to see who could take the seat of power ahead of their rival.

Al Sharpton immediately saw the delicacy of the situation.

Charles Taylor was really negotiating for an escape route that would allow him and his family to avoid execution and give him safe transit out of the country before the rival gangs could get their hands on him.

In contrast, the rival gangs wanted Sharpton to give his blessing to one gang over the other and to negotiate a cease-fire so that Sharpton's choice could begin to rule the country.

Sharpton was in an impossible situation because each faction passionately believed in its right to control the government. Perhaps even worse, the two factions were united in their desire for retribution against Taylor and they would not be happy unless Taylor became a corpse as proof that the old regime was truly dead.

Sharpton was brilliant and confounding all at the same time. Carlson despised his ways but admired the man.

As the hours dragged on, Sharpton engaged in shuttle diplomacy going between three rooms like Henry Kissinger seeking common ground between the groups. It really was a tribute to Sharpton's credibility that the three groups came to that hotel to patiently participate in this peace process.

Sharpton was even able to communicate with Secretary of State Colin Powell by telephone during this process and the groups realized that Sharpton was well connected.

Amazingly, slow progress was being achieved, even if the only form of that progress was the creation of a dialogue.

That was a good sign given that bloodlust seemed to be the universal goal prior to this conference.

As time went on, it was clear that Taylor merely wanted to leave the country with his wife and children and had given up on the idea of retaining any power whatsoever. Taylor realized that the two warring factions were both intent on torturing him and killing his family. A victory for Taylor would involve escape to a safe nation.

Given this, Sharpton actually created the outline of a workable agreement. Taylor would relinquish all governmental power to a new government comprised of representatives from each of the warring factions. Taylor would then exit the country with his wife and children leaving the factions to set up their own government.

There was one catch and it was a mighty big one. This plan could only be implemented if American troops entered Liberia to enforce its terms. Taylor was painfully aware of the fact that the white hot anger of both factions would prohibit his safe exit absent American troops to guarantee his departure unmolested.

It was also apparent to Sharpton that without American intervention, the two factions would slaughter each other and slaughter anyone associated with the opponents of their particular faction.

Sharpton could see that any solution he created was no solution at all if it continued to lead to further bloodshed.

Sharpton did have friends in high places in the American government, speaking frequently and desperately to Secretary of State Colin Powell. This was pretty impressive.

Sharpton assumed that Powell would be helpful out of a sense of racial solidarity. America's first black Secretary of

State, reasoned Sharpton, would not deny his black brother attempting to make history as a peace negotiator.

This was a terrible miscalculation by Sharpton. Powell was loath to commit American troops to further exposure given the expansive deployment of American soldiers all over the world and especially in various hotspots in the Middle East. Powell turned him down flat.

In the end, it never really mattered because the warring factions refused to accept any terms that involved safe passage out of the country for Taylor.

The peacekeeping mission was now officially shut down and the remainder of the trip turned into kind of a sightseeing expedition checking out many of the beautiful and historic locations in that part of Africa.

Carlson observed that Sharpton was disappointed but not defeated. Sharpton told him that pursuing peace was always a noble endeavor even when it's not successful. Sharpton told his traveling retinue that he would live to fight another day for other causes of justice and peace that would come down the pike in the future.

Even though he had not really conquered anything, Sharpton returned to America like a conquering hero and used this experience as a campaign highlight for his presidential run in 2004. Carlson admired the way that Sharpton could squeeze a little victory out of a dismal defeat.

Carlson was just happy to be home safe and sound. He loved to write about exciting things but he wanted to spend some time figuring out what America was all about.

Carlson the writer turned the Sharpton experience in Liberia into a very long article published in *Esquire*. The piece received rave reviews from all quarters.

If you get a chance, look for this article which was titled

"The League of Extraordinary Gentlemen" published in 2003. Carlson's style is amusing with a kind of homespun flair reminiscent of Mark Twain.

Charles Taylor did indeed make his escape into exile in Nigeria. However, he was eventually tried for war crimes in *The Hague* and is serving a fifty- year sentence.

The Liberian escapade and the ensuing article authored by Tucker really established once and for all that Carlson was a great writer.

Time would tell if Carlson could convert that skill into something television viewers would seek out in the future.

CHAPTER 13
NOT AFRAID TO HELP

E ver since Tucker Carlson accepted the mantle of responsibility from Bill O'Reilly in taking over the 8 o'clock hour, Carlson upped his level of courage by using that hour to come to the aid of persons mercilessly attacked by the mainstream media.

What happened is that Tucker Carlson engaged in in-depth research related to major litigation and if he discovered that the little guy was in danger of being unfairly crushed by the power of the state, Carlson would rush in like a SWAT team to rescue the victim and carry him off to safety.

This takes a lot of guts because the government doesn't like it when television hosts take sides against prosecuting attorneys. Whether you're coming from the right or the left, most broadcasters will stay out of the fray and merely tell the viewers that the best thing to do is simply wait until the trial is over before passing judgment.

In some cases, broadcasters will, in an attempt to cozy up to government officials, aggressively take the side of the prosecuting attorney. Frequently it's pretty blatant when some underfunded and outgunned citizen discovers that just about all of the television pundits are piling on to emphasize the obviousness of the alleged offender's guilt.

It makes you wonder if some TV host is merely hoping to avoid a tax audit by telegraphing authorities that they are on the government's side.

Tucker Carlson is absolutely fearless when it comes to this situation. Tucker despises criminal behavior as vigorously as the next guy if not even more so. However, his journalistic instincts will occasionally smell severe injustice and when that happens, he will use the bully pulpit of his vastly superior television program to lend aid to the innocent downtrodden defendant.

There are three major examples that demonstrate Tucker Carlson's willingness to put on the armor of justice when necessary.

The first one is Roger Stone.

Roger Stone was a very well-known political operative in the nation's capital. Throughout his life he was attracted to political campaigns and the thrill of political victory. In elementary school he campaigned for John F. Kennedy. Stone's family was devout Catholic and the idea of seeing a Catholic in the White House was exciting. Even at that young age, he was scheming to help his candidate, telling the other students that a vote for Nixon was a vote for extending the school week to include Saturdays.

As Stone grew older, he was drawn to more conservative politics and volunteered for the Barry Goldwater presidential campaign in 1964.

As a college student, he headed up the Young Republicans Club at George Washington University and invited a staff member from the Nixon team to address the group. This relationship expanded into a campaign job with the Nixon team.

With Nixon's victory, he began billing himself as a professional political consultant and worked on presidential campaigns throughout the remainder of his life always on the Republican side. He experienced a few losses but also enjoyed constructing victories for Ronald Reagan, George W. Bush, and Donald Trump.

Serious trouble came into his life when special prosecutor Robert Mueller attempted to obtain evidence against President Donald Trump related to the Russia investigation. A jury eventually convicted him of various crimes related to the probe conducted by Congress and by the Mueller team.

Tucker smelled a rat from the very beginning of the Stone prosecution. Stone had no previous criminal record and no history of violence. In fact, his alleged crimes had nothing to do with violent actions. Despite this, the special prosecutor arrested Stone at his home in the middle of the night with swarms of armored SWAT teams swooping in as if John Dillinger had been caught.

Carlson also found it suspicious that the FBI had tipped off CNN so that the entire humiliating arrest of Roger Stone in his pajamas could be broadcast to the entire nation.

Carlson took Stone's side not just because he thought he might be innocent but because Carlson knew that the Russian case was a gigantic hoax perpetrated by the Hillary Clinton campaign creating fake information used as a pretense to stop Trump's election.

Carlson found it repulsive that a 70 year-old man could be dragged away in the middle of the night accused of impeding an investigation illegal from its inception by the FBI's desire to fabricate a connection between Russia and the Trump campaign.

Carlson realized that the Stone prosecution was a Stalinist attempt to destroy one's political enemies through manipulation of the criminal justice system.

For this reason, Carlson night after night on his TV show hammered away at the bizarre acts of injustice in the way that the Stone case was handled.

Long before the *Durham Report* explained widespread abuse in an FBI that had been turned into an extension of the Hillary Clinton campaign, Carlson saw that the entire attack against Stone reeked of the rotting flesh of corrupt federal law enforcement.

Carlson reran the footage of Stone's late-night arrest to emphasize the unfair behavior of Federal officials. He then put one guest after another in front of the cameras to unmask the truth of what was happening. At one point in the process, Roger Stone himself appeared on the program to give his side of the story.

Stone's conviction did not stall Carlson's ardent defense of this Republican operative. It was obvious to Carlson that since Mueller's report found no crime on the part of Trump, it was a horrible injustice to seek incarceration of an old man convicted of lying about a nonexistent crime.

Stone was eventually pardoned by President Trump in order to save him from the 40-month sentence that was sure to either shorten Stone's life or maybe even kill him if carried out.

Taking on the FBI and the entire Federal justice system is not for the faint of heart. Carlson did it anyway as a matter of moral principle. That took some guts.

The next example is the case of Michael Flynn. Flynn was

a retired Lieutenant General in the United States Army with significant experience in Afghanistan and Iraq. He was pegged as President Trump's National Security Advisor shortly after Trump's election victory in 2016.

He was then forced to resign amid accusations that he lied to FBI agents in relation to his communications with Russian ambassador Sergey Kislyak.

The only crime pressed against Michael Flynn was that he was untruthful talking to agents investigating Flynn's conversation with the Russian leader.

FBI Director James Comey sent agents over to the White House to engage in friendly questioning with reference to the conversation with the Russian. Comey directed the agents to put Flynn at ease so that Flynn would lower his guard and offer some kind of contradiction in his statements.

Comey disliked Trump and wanted to find a way to cause political injury to his new boss. James Comey was disappointed when the agents returned to headquarters reporting Michael Flynn had been truthful. FBI Director Comey then assembled a team to review the notes compiled by the agents that had interviewed Flynn. He directed them to find the crime by identifying some trivial contradiction.

They did as ordered.

That was all that was needed. Comey initiated Federal charges against General Flynn.

General Flynn was terrified by what was happening and resigned his post as National Security Director. He then hired high-priced attorneys who presented Flynn with a plea deal that he was forced to accept despite his innocence. The Federal prosecutors threatened further prosecution of members of Flynn's family if Flynn refused the deal.

Flynn was a family man who realized that he had to fall on his sword to protect his loved ones.

Tucker Carlson again to the rescue. Prior to sentencing, Flynn hired new lawyers who uncovered the rats at FBI headquarters. The Federal Judge overseeing the case fought hard to keep the truth from the public and to make sure that General Flynn was locked away so that the secret deceptions of the FBI could never be revealed.

Carlson was having none of it. This case, like the Roger Stone prosecution, was a clear-cut case of attacking Trump through the public humiliation of one of his key appointments.

Carlson found it especially distressing because it demonstrated that the Director of the FBI had no more scruples than a third world dictator solving political problems by destroying his enemies.

The Trump administration was handcuffed from day one by the sense of fear that pervaded everyone who worked for Trump. The message was clear: if you are loyal to the President then you can become an FBI target regardless of your innocence.

Carlson took to the airwaves and put Michael Flynn's attorneys front and center to expose the way the FBI created crimes out of whole cloth in order to bring down the President.

Carlson however, would not be intimidated and word of Carlson's courage was circulating in conservative circles. A lot of Trump supporters began to worry about Carlson himself becoming an FBI target. The sense of fear was everywhere in Trump circles.

After Trump fired the FBI director, James Comey appeared on a television talk show and laughed about the way his FBI agents had deceived General Flynn and the way the general was vulnerable to Comey's scheme. Comey's behavior, criminal in nature, was entertaining to the former FBI director.

Carlson wasn't afraid to tell the world the truth about Flynn and wasn't afraid to tell the world that Jim Comey was dedicated to shredding the Constitution in the name of politics. Jim Comey did not think Trump should be president and he was willing to use any tactic at his disposal to bring down the Trump administration.

It was truly frightening: Tucker Carlson was one of the few media pundits willing to speak truth to power.

The last example of Carlson's using his powerful microphone to protect the little guy against evil prosecutors involved the case of Kyle Rittenhouse.

Kyle Rittenhouse was a 17-year-old student who traveled from his home in Antioch, Illinois to Kenosha Wisconsin for the explicit purpose of protecting people and property from BLM rioters destroying businesses throughout the Kenosha area.

Rittenhouse was attacked by some of the rioters and was forced to discharge his weapon in order to defend his own life.

Rittenhouse was placed on trial for murdering two of the rioters and wounding another. The case became a *cause célèbre* for those seeking racial justice. Rittenhouse was accused of being a white supremacist and soon thereafter the trial became a national story with reporters detailing every development that occurred.

Tucker Carlson took an interest in the story because his researchers were uncovering certain facts inconsistent with the narrative put forward by the mainstream media.

Carlson told his audience that this story could not be about race because the people shot by Rittenhouse were also white just like Rittenhouse.

In addition, Carlson objected to the idea that self-defense was portrayed as inappropriate because the attackers were demonstrating as part of a protest against police racism.

Carlson agreed that Rittenhouse exercised poor judgment in going to Kenosha to protect the community against the violent protesters. But Carlson also argued that shooting someone who's trying to kill you is a justified act.

For this reason, Carlson bravely took up the cause of Kyle Rittenhouse when virtually no one else in the media was willing to do so.

The general narrative in the broadcast media, print media, and the other cable networks was that Kyle Rittenhouse was a racist who intentionally intervened in the Kenosha riots in an effort to seek out and kill black people.

Carlson presented the evidence dispassionately as it was given to the jury during the trial. He told his audience that it would be a shocking miscarriage of justice for this foolish young man to be convicted of murder when he was merely trying to defend himself.

This took a lot of chutzpah for Carlson to take this viewpoint. Civil rights leaders urged advertisers to abandon the Tucker Carlson show. Intense pressure was put on Fox News to silence Tucker's defense of Rittenhouse. Throughout the national media, Tucker Carlson was described as a Klansman seeking justification of racial violence.

In the end, Rittenhouse, and therefore indirectly Carlson were vindicated by the jury verdict declaring the 17-year-old not guilty on all counts.

When Carlson proclaimed the verdict a victory of justice

The media fed Rittenhouse to the wolves until Tucker and the jury came to the rescue.

over a media mob hungry to consume the blood of a young racist, the truth of what really happened emerged.

The entire country was stunned to learn that almost the entire media and left-wing pundits had been lying about the Rittenhouse case from the beginning. Trial testimony was not being broadcast to show the truth of what had actually happened. The most shocking testimony ignored by most media came from one of the wounded rioters who admitted that he had pointed a loaded gun at Rittenhouse's head.

Carlson was visibly relieved to see that somehow justice had been served. Perhaps one of the most moving interviews in the history of television occurred when Rittenhouse agreed to give Carlson first crack at a post-trial television interview.

Carlson was grateful for the coup of getting the Rittenhouse interview. But Rittenhouse was even more grateful because he realized that Carlson had been in his corner from the beginning. The Truth is that Carlson wasn't in Rittenhouse's corner for any reason other than that the evidence showed Rittenhouse to be innocent. Carlson's team had done a superb job of assembling the true facts that allowed Carlson to pick up and carry the banner of justice on behalf of Rittenhouse.

After that initial interview, Carlson conducted a moving longform hour interview with Rittenhouse as part of a brand-new Tucker Carlson product called *Tucker Carlson Originals.*

This new longform discussion was created by Carlson to provide a more in-depth understanding of a story which could not be conveyed in your standard five-minute quick hit interview.

The long form interview provided all the little details supporting Carlson's decision to expose the Rittenhouse prosecution as the government bowing to public opinion, indicting the innocent.

Tucker Carlson was now riding high on a wave of success where he was perceived as a man of morality willing to take broadcast risks to protect the innocent.

All of the world, broadcast personalities, and the average Joe on the street began to realize that Tucker Carlson was willing to go to the mat to help the lonely target of injustice if he could.

Tucker Carlson was developing into some sort of superhero, a Superman who stood for truth, justice, and the American way.

CHAPTER 14
SEX ABUSE TARGET

One of the things about Tucker Carlson that makes him sort of endearing is that despite his great success in some areas of life he comes across as a normal red-blooded American guy.

By that I mean that Tucker Carlson occasionally says something with a sexual implication in a slightly humorous way. It's never directed to anyone on his staff and he certainly is not known to come on to female employees or guests. By all accounts, Tucker Carlson is a very happily married man who enjoys the affections and intimacy of his beautiful wife.

He does on occasion however say something that lets you know that he is a vibrant specimen of American manhood where testosterone occupies its proper lane in the healthy blood flowing through his veins.

What I'm trying to say is that this healthy father and husband is a real guy kind of like most guys.

We live in a world where media personalities and high-profile officials keep their guard up so constantly that you sometimes wonder if there is a pulse in some of these men. A great example is former Vice-president Mike Pence who is so skittish about saying or doing something that might be misinterpreted in relation to any woman not his wife, that he simply refuses to be alone in any room with a woman other than his wife. This is the way Mike Pence insulates himself against accusations of sexual impropriety.

Since the inception of the *Me Too* movement, the American male frequently guards his speech and demeanor around women, lest he be accused of something improper.

Mike pence has taken this to the extreme of course but who can blame him?

Donald Trump denies taking liberties with beautiful women but nonetheless paid a steep price for his locker room braggadocio in which he told an *Entertainment Tonight* host that he could freely grab women by their genitals without repercussion.

Trump thought the remark was private but has been famously excoriated as a sexual predator since it was made public.

The point here is that guys sometimes say things that they shouldn't say as a function of their raw untamed masculinity. In today's world, all of us try to refrain from these statements out of a sense of propriety and respect for women.

There's an old song from the 1940s titled *"Standing On The Corner"*. The chorus intones "just standing on the corner watching all the girls go by". During the verse the male protagonists sings "you can't go to jail for what you're thinking."

The truth though is that in the modern world of cancel culture, you could lose your job or an election or maybe even your reputation if you give voice to thoughts initiated by your male libido.

Tucker Carlson however has a very good record as it relates to women. Still, you can tell that he is a real guys' guy and this makes him relatable to his male viewers.

An outtake from his Fox television show shows him discussing one of his political foils in an off-air comment. Tucker can be heard describing the man's wife as "yummy". Tucker is seen immediately realizing that tape was rolling during his comment and he quickly indicates that he never met the woman but also realizes some of his enemies would try to use the comment against him if they ever got their hands on the tape.

On another occasion, as Tucker prepared to go live with an interview with Piers Morgan, he engaged in a brief repartee off air as technicians made final arrangements for the interview. As a joke, Tucker tells Piers that the upcoming interview might be more interesting if the two men talked about sexual techniques with their respective spouses instead of focusing on the political issues of the day. Morgan enjoyed the joke and the two men conducted a right and proper interview as soon as the red light went on.

Afterwards, some who obtained access to the pre-interview dialogue between the men described Tucker as a person who creates a sexist environment onset.

The truth is that Tucker occasionally acts like a normal human. This means that he might say something off-color as a form of casual expression. Tucker is not sexist and certainly does not have any predatory leanings.

Every woman who has worked with him through these many years describes him as polite, respectful, and fun to work with. Tucker is comfortable in his own skin and sees no need to construct Mike Pence style barriers to communication with the fairer sex.

Unfortunately, appearing on television on a regular basis increases your public profile so significantly that you can become a target for those wanting to ruin your reputation even if you live a life of faithfulness to your marriage.

Here's a story that few people know but that most of us can relate to when it comes to experiencing real fear.

Because the *Me Too* movement presses forward with a slogan of "believe all women", the idea that a mere accusation of sexual impropriety, no matter how absurd, can ruin your life irreparably is not too far-fetched.

Tucker Carlson was a victim of a fictitious accusation that almost boiled over into a career-killing headline.

While Tucker was working as cohost of the PBS discussion show called *Crossfire*, he received a letter from an attorney accusing Carlson of raping his client in a restaurant-bar called *Harper's Restaurant* in Louisville, Kentucky. The correspondent told Carlson that the attorney would be filing criminal sex charges within a few days of the letter. The lawyer also invited Carlson to generate a response to the accusation.

Carlson was dumbstruck. The accuser, named Kimberly Carter, even identified a specific date and time for the alleged crime.

Carlson immediately identified all of it as a lie. Carlson not only had not been to Louisville on the date in question, but Carlson had never even visited the state of Kentucky at any time in his life.

Despite this, he was nervous and was losing sleep regarding this complete fabrication. After all, the letter itself was real and it came from an actual licensed attorney.

Bob Bennett, the attorney who defended Bill Clinton

during the Monica Lewinsky affair, jumped into help Carlson snuff out this outrageous lie.

Bennett and Carlson took a gamble as a shortcut method to end this crisis. Carlson, on Bennett's advice, agreed to sit for a polygraph test with a gentleman retired from the FBI as one of the bureau's chief polygraph experts.

It was a gut-wrenching polygraph examination which took almost 2 hours to administer. Carlson was nervous throughout the entire process, afraid that the adrenaline of fear flowing through his veins would send the polygraph needles spiking even though he was truthful throughout the exam.

The questions were tricky such as "have you ever dreamed of having sex with a woman who is not your wife"? Answering questions about his sex fantasy dreams in front of a hard-boiled former FBI Special agent was almost too much for him to bear.

Fortunately for Carlson, the polygraph expert was an honest man just doing his job. Carlson passed the polygraph with flying colors.

In addition, Carlson's lawyers provided specific evidence demonstrating more than just an alibi. They proved that Carlson had never been in Kentucky and certainly had never been in Harper's Restaurant. Carlson proved that he was in Washington, DC taping *Crossfire* during the period in which the rape was supposed to have occurred.

The good news is that the allegations never became public. Carlson's career would live on.

The entire incident however, gave Tucker Carlson pause. As part of his job, he was constantly chasing down rumors and innuendos mostly about political figures. He saw the devastating effect of false allegations that ruined lives and destroyed marriages.

Carlson ruminated about the way Congressman Gary Condit's career came crashing down amid rumors that he may have murdered a young intern who had worked in his office. The intern's family and the District of Columbia Police Department fanned the flames of the story despite the lack of evidence. The news media went into a frenzy of 24/7 coverage.

It did not help Congressman Condit that he had in fact had a brief affair with the intern.

Armies of CNN investigators and police detectives could not find any evidence connecting the Congressman with the murder. Condit was soundly defeated by a virtual unknown in his next reelection bid. All because the world had been convinced that Condit was a murderer.

A couple of years later, the intern's body was recovered in a park and an itinerant vagrant confessed to the murder.

The actual truth barely made a ripple in the media. The entire thing had been a lie but Condit faded into obscurity, a victim of the media's lust for a big story.

Kimberly Carter admitted she was suffering from delusions that caused her to falsely accuse Tucker Carlson.

Carlson, having survived the false accusations of Kimberly Carter, came away from the experience with a newfound appreciation for those that live a public life.

He realized that the delicate operation of dismantling a false charge could easily blow up in your face. Just as a bomb expert carefully diffuses an explosive, protecting your reputation in the face of a nasty lie is not such an easy thing.

Tucker Carlson heaved a huge sigh of relief as the Kimberly Carter matter faded into the background of his life. Being a public figure can sometimes be dangerous, and Kimberly Carter almost turned Tucker Carlson into a dead man.

CHAPTER 15
BEANS

There is a very popular television host, podcaster, and author by the name of Mike Rowe who sings the virtues of working-class people. Mike Rowe for years has been trying to drive home the idea that our greatest achievers and folks that are most to be admired are the people who use their brawn as well as their brain to make their way in the world.

His very popular television program *Dirty Jobs* is designed to show that there is honor in completion of a hard day's work even when that work involves the sweat of your brow and might leave you with an aching back at the end of the day.

As part of these efforts, Mike Rowe has also demonstrated that financial success and independence frequently come to those that learn a trade as an alternative to four years of college that leads to insurmountable debt and a sheepskin that is of no particular interest to hiring authorities.

Mike Rowe is revolutionizing the way we think about work and labor. He is proving to the world that the people who truly get things done are those that use their hands to manipulate a wide variety of resources in providing service or in creating the things that keep the world spinning.

The overarching message from Mike Rowe however, is the message of dignity. Highbrow intellectuals in their ivory towers often contribute little or nothing to our society while the grunt work undertaken by contractors and service providers is what truly grows our economy and makes life more livable for all of mankind.

Mike Rowe is not opposed to college but he does believe the pathway to success for the young and ambitious need not be found on a university campus. In fact, Mike Rowe recognizes that many universities are merely a super expensive cesspool of pseudo-intellectuals filled with ingratitude for the opportunities given to them by this country.

Mike Rowe finds dignity in dirty jobs. So does Tucker Carlson.

Podcast sensation Adam Carolla adheres to this school of thought as well. Corolla grew up in a welfare environment but emerged into the sunlight of success through the backbreaking work of construction sites.

He eventually became a media star but he continually preaches about the value of challenging physical labor. It's clear that his success in media would never have materialized without the lesson that there is great dignity in hard work.

This is where Tucker Carlson comes into the picture. Tucker Carlson grew up in the lap of luxury going to high-level boarding schools and then on to Trinity College for a degree in history.

Tucker has had every opportunity to avoid manual labor and to live his work life strictly in an office environment where the only opportunity to get your hands dirty might be in changing the toner cartridge for the copy machine.

But that really is not what Tucker Carlson is about.

He has a real appreciation for the working stiff who comes home every day with all the body aches and calluses that come from a real hard day's work. He truly appreciates that writing and broadcasting rarely involve the kind of filth and physical exertion typical for tradesmen and service workers.

A great example of this is included in his Book called *The Great Slide*. In this tome, Carlson describes the way that he and one of his buddies obtained a last-minute summer job working for a company that made baked beans in tin cans.

He describes his various duties at baked beans central in excruciating detail. He found himself frequently coated with various parts of the baked bean sauce recipe that might be delicious when properly diluted and mixed with all the delicious beans. However, the substances frequently had an acidic effect on his skin and clothes and even his hair.

The substances also were known to cause a semi-permanent change in color to the human epidermis as these chemical-like gelatinous ingredients tended to penetrate anything they came in contact with, leaving everything with a new hue.

Carlson marveled at the magnificent scale of the production facilities at the baked beans factory. He describes gigantic pots the size of your living room where the old-style tradition of cooking beans in a pot was well preserved. Never mind that an accurate reenactment of the old tradition involved a 3-gallon pot as opposed to the 44,000 gallon pot that was heavy and unwieldy for those working for the bean magnates.

Especially entertaining is Tucker's description of his special assignment as destroyer of damaged cans of beans. Management realized that it was too risky for consumers to be allowed to purchase cans of beans occasionally too damaged for sale. Management also realized that they could be faced with significant personal injury liability if those damaged cans somehow left the factory and found their way into circulation in the general populace.

That's where the can destroyers come in. The can destroyer was equipped with a gigantic handheld spike which was to be plunged into the defective can of beans in order to make sure that the guilty can of beans would never see anyone's kitchen table.

Eventually that summer, Tucker Carlson was rotated from the cooking department to the can destruction department. With a sort of sick delight, Carlson describes his violent duty plunging the stainless steel spike into the ill-fated cans, beans and sauce shooting out of the can from the point of spike entry.

Bean excrement shot out everywhere in a special room designed for this violent display. Tucker, bean executioner extraordinaire, covered from head to toe in cold beans and sauce, actually enjoyed the experience.

The point in all of this is to show that Tucker happily blended in with all the other bean folk, making a number of friends along the way and demonstrating to anyone that was willing to take notice that Tucker Carlson was no elitist turning his nose up at those who worked in disgusting low-paid jobs.

Going forward in his life, Tucker Carlson would have

empathy for the working man and woman. And would never talk down to them or show them disrespect.

In fact, despite his pedigree, Tucker Carlson Carlson's most loyal audience consists of the blue-collar lunch bucket crowd who recognizes that Tucker has their back.

When Tucker says that he relates to the average American worker, he is speaking from experience.

He still has little traces of barbecue sauce bonded to his cuticles.

CHAPTER 16
INSURRECTION

The President was obviously unhappy with the election results. To him, it was a matter of national pride that true patriots would not be hoodwinked by the scam perpetrated on the nation. Clearly government authorities were working against him and he even had an inkling at that time that agencies of the national government had been plotting to bring about an illegitimate vote.

Despite his anger, he did not want his followers to storm the Capitol building. He truly wanted electoral justice but realized he was in no position to bring that about himself and he knew that some form of physical disruption would not prove to be a winning strategy. The president hoped to pursue political and litigation means to achieve a truly just result.

A small handful of protesters however, were not willing to abide the unjust and misleading electoral outcome. They felt that the only way to properly focus world attention on the rigged nature of the election would be to enter the building while the legislature was in session.

They knew it would be tricky but they also knew that with so much commotion going on they might be able to find their way into the legislative chambers while Congress was in session.

Having negotiated their way past security, four of these protesters found themselves on the famous patterned blue carpet on the floor of the United States House of Representatives. They unfurled a large banner of protest as the representatives debated various matters between themselves.

They screamed for justice at the top of their lungs and slowly across the room there was spreading awareness that something unusual was happening in the chambers. At first, the congressmen became quiet, waiting to see what the protesters would do next. It was then that their leader produced a pistol and began shooting.

Chaos reigned in the Capitol for the next several minutes with bullets flying and Congressional staffers diving for cover.

Capitol Hill police converged on the quartet of protesters but not before serious damage had been done. Five congressmen had been shot and all five were attended by their fellow legislators, congressional pages, and Capitol Hill police with EMT training.

The year was 1954.

The four protesters were part of the Puerto Rican Nationalist movement angry over a fake election conducted by the United States to show the world that Puerto Rico chose to be a subset of the United States.

They knew the election had been rigged with deceptive wording to convince Puerto Ricans that their association with the United States would not destroy their ability to self-govern. The Nationalists saw that Puerto Ricans had voted against independence only because of lies coming out of Washington.

The former president of the Puerto Rican Nationalist Party who inspired the protesters was Don Pedro Albizu Campos, who corresponded with the protesters from his prison cell. He vociferously objected to the fake election and the way its results were being used as propaganda against those who truly wanted complete independence for this Caribbean nation.

The Nationalists protesters stormed the Capitol brandishing their pistols, led by a mysterious and beautiful dark-haired fair skinned woman by the name of Lolita Lebron. She was a young 34 year old firebrand from San Juan determined to free the island nation from the shackles of Washington politicians.

Lebron and her cohorts were clearly determined to use violence as a way to get America to reverse course in its domination of Puerto Rico.

This was a real insurrection.

The kind of effort where violence and death were used to coerce from government leaders the outcome desired by the seditious thugs.

Lovely Lolita Lebron's insurrection featured firing guns in the Capitol in 1954.

The four insurgents were quickly convicted in front of a federal jury of "trying to overthrow the government of the United States".

America had survived this, the only insurrectionist attack on the Capitol prior to January 6, 2021.

In 1979 President Jimmy Carter commuted the sentences of all the perpetrators who otherwise would've died in prison to serve out the 75 year sentence handed down by the judge.

The insurrectionists received a hero's welcome in San Juan upon prison release. Lolita Lebron, even after all those years, was not penitent.

A person in the crowd asked Lolita why she fired pistols in the Capitol. She smiled and responded **"if you're not firing weapons, it's not really an insurrection"**.

She was right.

CHAPTER 17
JANUARY 6 TAPES

After one of the most disputed campaigns to become Speaker Of The House, Congressman Kevin McCarthy wore the battle scars from the competition.

The mainstream press criticized his inability to accumulate the Republican votes needed for a first ballot victory. They said the protracted floor debate diminished his ability to lead the house with authority.

Some even described him as emasculated after several conservatives accused him of lacking true conservative credentials.

McCarthy needed a powerful restorative.

Something to put him back on top of the Republican Party. After all, with Trump out of office, McCarthy was the highest ranking Republican elected official in the federal government.

He needed to get back his mojo.

Ousted Speaker Nancy Pelosi enjoyed the spectacle of division in the Republican ranks. She had occasionally been challenged for the speakership when the Democrats had the congressional majority, but she swiftly dispatched two challengers who were wiped off the board on the first ballot. She knew how to punish defectors. She knew how to wield power.

She gloated.

McCarthy was now The Speaker of The House, third in line for the presidency, but to Pelosi and the Democrats, he was a paper tiger, ill-equipped to wear the congressional crown.

Viewing McCarthy a wimp surrounded by sharks like Matt Gaetz and Lauren Bober, some arch-conservatives were not willing to tolerate McCarthy's leadership.

Pelosi on the other hand, had demanded fealty during her tenure. And she got it under penalty of political death.

McCarthy... not so much.

Even some in conservative media felt that the prolonged opposition to McCarthy rendered his speakership dead on arrival. After all, how could he build a coalition to pass a Republican agenda when he couldn't assemble the needed votes on the first ballot. There were too many vocal opponents within the Republican caucus to weave together moderate Republicans and hard right bomb throwers.

Democrats relished the image of a dysfunctional Republican congressional caucus.

Although McCarthy pooh-poohed the idea of dissension in the ranks, he knew that he needed help to get out of the gate. He didn't want to be seen limping onto the main stage in American politics. He needed a reversal of fortune.

He needed what the Greek playwrights called the *Deus Ex Machina*. He needed to plant a flag declaring his authority, restoring respect, instantly installing confidence in his leadership.

Something powerful. Something bold.

He had a plan.

He had the tapes.

Not actual tapes but the video.

The raw video footage of the events of January 6, 2021. Over 44,000 hours of digital video footage gathered from over 296 cameras catching every movement of every human who crossed into the sphere of each camera lens on that fateful day of January 6 AKA "The Insurrection".

The special *January 6 Committee* was convened by Speaker Pelosi to conduct a show trial seeking convictions in the court of public opinion. The committee presented well-orchestrated productions highlighting bad behavior by Trump supporters as Congress was meeting to certify the Biden presidential victory.

And it made for compelling television, the *January 6 Committee* even hiring a major TV network executive to serve as producer of the prime-time kangaroo court.

With ABC Television's Jim Goldston directing the Democrats' play, it was obvious that video segments would be central to this stage show in between witness testimony. The Committee emphasized the severity of the violence and the motivation of those that entered the Capitol.

The video clips told the story of crazed opponents of democracy seeking scalps and the installation of King Trump in the throne room of the presidency.

The Committee, composed of only Democrats and Trump-hating Republicans handpicked by Pelosi, wanted America to see Trump supporters seeking violent overthrow of the American Republic.

The Committee used highlight reels to paint Trump as a Third World Generalissimo sending his goons into the capital to restore his junta to power.

Video clips seemed to do the trick. Commentators were horrified by the videos, especially when they were narrated by former Trumpers, now penitent after convictions in federal court.

These witnesses were ashamed of their behavior, but said Trump drove them to it with his fiery words on the Ellipse preceding the mob entering the Capitol building.

Now that McCarthy was Speaker Of The House, he got a feeling that he could rehabilitate his reputation by taking a huge gamble. Since he now controlled the January 6 raw video footage, would that footage possibly contain images exonerating the alleged insurrectionists?

Could McCarthy single-handedly change the score of the public perception ballgame by revealing the January 6 videos in the full context of the complete video unedited?

If he could, and if the complete video was exonerating, he would be a hero to the hardliners that opposed his nomination as speaker and would truly elevate his standing in the Republican Party. The tapes could help him certify his *Bona Fides* with conservative Americans suspicious that McCarthy was a Republican in name only.

He was willing to gamble. He was willing to release the raw video footage that Pelosi had kept under lock and key.

McCarthy surmised that the January 6 Committee only showed short video segments because the full video showed not so much a mob but rather a bunch of folks wandering and loitering, discovering a chance to sightsee after entering the building.

But it was a big gamble: if he guessed wrong, he was feeding the insurrection narrative and would further damage his stock with conservatives and with former President Trump.

Speaker McCarthy ponders: To release or not to release, that is the question...

The new speaker had an inkling that the tapes would tell a dramatically different tale that would contrast with the January 6 committee's narrative.

He saw that Pelosi and company aggressively prohibited access to the full footage. Even members of Congress were prevented from viewing the full camera data.

Why?

McCarthy was about to place a big bet on the house, figuratively and literally speaking.

So he decided to release all of the footage, over strenuous objections from committee members.

Congressman Adam Schiff said the release would threaten national security. Trump-hating Congressman Adam Kinzinger accused McCarthy of risking congressional safety by revealing the location of hidden cameras.

Capitol Hill police were forced to obey the speaker's orders and gave all the video to McCarthy, with certain conditions. McCarthy complied with those conditions using technology to blur certain faces and deleting data to protect privacy and security concerns of the Capitol Hill police.

Despite these precautions, Democrats insisted on secrecy for the videos saying McCarthy had a callous disregard for the safety and welfare of sitting Congressmen.

The stage was set. McCarthy was ready to execute his plan. Ready to call the bet in this high-stakes poker game. He was ready to release all the video for all the world to see.

But how would he do it? The most obvious choice would be to distribute the digital images in a file given every media outlet on earth and to anyone who asked. He would simply designate the videos as a public record subject to anyone's scrutiny.

Logical.

Effective.

But... there was another option. Another way to do it.

He could give the raw video footage to just one person: Tucker Carlson.

Tucker Carlson was the most celebrated voice of conservative thought on the planet.

And Tucker Carlson had the resources: a gigantic staff who could watch the 44,000 hours of raw footage and compare it to the *January 6 Committee* narrative.

McCarthy needed the video for his redemption but that redemption would depend on the one man in the world who could digest the video, take it apart, and present it in context.

If the video contained the truth.

It was a huge gamble.

The question remaining was this: if McCarthy picks Tucker Carlson as the one and only recipient of McCarthy's cache of January 6 video, would Tucker be able to handle it? Could he find the truth, and deliver it to the American people?

McCarthy's career depended on it.

Carlson's career depended on it.

In some ways, the integrity of the American government depended on it.

Then, Tucker Carlson delivered.

On February 26, 2023, McCarthy instructed his Chief of Staff to hand carry a box containing 10 thumb drives. Two Capitol Hill policemen accompanied the Speaker's Chief of Staff to the airport where the delivery team took the box of thumb drives to the headquarters of Fox News in New York City. Instructions were very specific.

The box had to be delivered personally into the hands of Tucker Carlson himself. He signed a receipt confirming successful delivery.

A buzz began throughout the Fox News media empire. What did the video contain? Speculation ran rampant.

Tucker himself hated the secrecy and the cloak and dagger stuff.

The pressure at Fox headquarters was intense. It was like you're holding the secret of eternal life but couldn't tell a soul.

Tucker had an idea but he had to confer with McCarthy.

Tucker asked that rather than take 10 days to have a staff review the material and then reveal the facts of the video and Tucker's analysis all at once, why not tell the world immediately that he had the tapes. Then Carlson would spend a week or so viewing and analyzing, shooting for a bombshell show that Tucker could promote as a big reveal?

McCarthy reluctantly okayed the plan and the next night, Tucker revealed that he had the video but the world would have to wait for the Carlson team to carefully and deliberately review the product to see what they had.

Democratic media leaders went ballistic. In Democratic leadership offices, a lawsuit asking for a restraining order was contemplated.

For Democrats, it wasn't about stopping McCarthy anymore as much as it was about stopping Tucker Carlson.

The pressure in Carlson's office subsided a little while they focused on an impossible task: viewing and evaluating 44,000 hours of video in preparation for what would be one of the most anticipated broadcasts in American history. And they had to complete the job within 10 days because Tucker had promised his audience that he would bring the project in under that short deadline.

While Carlson employees burned the midnight oil, the brass at Fox News was nervous.

Senior executives remembered the Al Capone safe debacle from years earlier. In 1986, ABC-TV spent a fortune promoting Geraldo Rivera's coverage of the opening of a safe belonging to long dead notorious gangster Al Capone. ABC and Rivera created "Capone Fever" as the mustachioed host and his network encouraged uncontrolled frenzy over the potential secrets within the gangster's impenetrable safe. Anticipation was unbelievable.

Finally, on live television the safe was opened to reveal… Nothing!

Empty!

Rivera was humiliated. ABC was embarrassed.

It was a complete debacle. Television news was damaged and would take a long time to recover. America felt ripped off and betrayed: tricked into watching a big nothing. Now, the Fox leaders prayed for something real instead of another Al Capone disaster.

On the night of March 6, 2023, Tucker Carlson broadcast to the world the January 6 video.

It was an instant success and more importantly a thunderous attack on the credibility of the *January 6 Committee*.

The tape showed hundreds of so-called insurrectionists in the role of sightseers in need of a tour guide. In fact, the video showed very little violence against police and security.

While the congressional *January 6 Committee* showed the tiny percentage of rabble who assaulted police, the committee ignored the 95% of the video capturing curious unarmed and most importantly docile protesters walking calmly throughout the building.

Tucker's most spectacular footage showed the horned Viking guy who'd been portrayed by the January 6 committee chairman as the "face of violent insurrection" respectfully following directions from Capitol Hill police as they unlocked doors throughout the complex upon his polite request.

One clip shows horn guy leading a prayer for God's protection upon the police and security. The man Democrats saw as the embodiment of terrorist armed rebellion came across as gentle and deferential toward authority.

At one point, he calmly sits in Pelosi's office and leaves her a note.

Carlson's video release fomented a snowstorm of motions from January 6 defendants previously convicted and those awaiting trial.

The Justice Department was now in trouble because Carlson was releasing video the prosecutors were otherwise required to give to the defendants' lawyers but had failed to do so.

The video was exculpatory, a legal term meaning supporting innocence.

The nation was outraged: the violent overthrow of our government was in actuality a tepid failure to keep protesters out of the building. Protesters in the released video were nonviolent loiterers. I've seen more aggression in the bleachers of a Cleveland Browns football game.

To be fair, some few of those who stormed the barricades that day went too far, and some police were assaulted. However, the *January 6 Committee* cherry-picked those video clips while attempting to bury the dominant true story of the day, namely, that disgruntled citizens wandered the Capitol without causing injury or damage.

Investigative reporter John Solomon even discovered that the January 6 Committee had audio dubbed onto video segments from cameras that had no microphones to begin with. In other words, silent video suddenly had accompanying audio because the committee *created it!*

McCarthy was vindicated. His gambit had paid off.

McCarthy remembered the words of Lolita Lebron when she was asked about the 1954 shooting at the U. S. Capitol. She had told the press that *"if you're not firing weapons, it's not really an insurrection".*

It wasn't really an insurrection.

Pelosi's was now seen as a liar and a grifter trying to pull the wool over the eyes of Americans. The entire *January 6 Committee* hearings were now viewed as a Soviet-style show trial led by comrades anxious to execute the treasonous who dared insult Joseph Stalin.

McCarthy now ascended to new heights in the eyes of many Americans. He had courageously pulled back the curtain to reveal a dead body still alive like a zombie seeking the death of your family.

Pelosi and company were revealed as destroyers of truth, employing any duplicity, no matter how disgusting, to further their aims to achieve political power.

Tucker Carlson, a mere mortal with a microphone and a TV show, had made it all possible. McCarthy himself understood as left-wing pundits scrambled for excuses, that Tucker Carlson had been the one person who could effectively get out the truth and rally Americans.

It's as if Carlson had created a truth militia: everyday folks from average middle American families were told the truth and refused to be cowed by the liars of the Democratic Party and the charlatans posing as objective journalists.

Tucker Carlson had not just vindicated McCarthy.

Carlson had also vindicated former President Donald Trump.

The January 6 Committee narrative actually had two objectives.

The first objective was to show the January 6 events as a violent insurrection designed to topple our democracy. This objective was trashed by the obviously peaceful behavior shown by the majority of citizens rambling around the Capitol as seen in the video.

The second objective and perhaps the core goal of the *January 6 Committee* was also stopped dead in its tracks through Carlson's program of March 6. The second objective was to portray Donald Trump himself as the ringleader and as director of an insurrection. Of course, Trump did not use words inciting violence or even trespass. He told his followers to "fight" the same way that Chuck Schumer and Barack Obama urged "fighting" against unjust policies.

However, Carlson's display of the videos destroyed all hope of making Trump the fall guy for the great insurrection.

After all, how could Trump be guilty of plotting and inciting a *coup d'état* if the boss's henchmen merely meandered through the halls of Congress aimlessly and unarmed.

In a single broadcasting blow, Tucker Carlson has saved the careers of both the speaker of the house and the former president.

True, McCarthy had handed the weapons to Carlson but only Tucker Carlson knew how to wield that sword. In one determined courageous broadcast Carlson proved that he was unique among conservative pundits.

At a time when traditional conservatives seemed incapable of standing against left-wing tyrants, Carlson never considered compromise. Carlson didn't give a fat rat's behind what the *New York Times* thought of him. Carlson was a sniper who didn't think twice when given the chance for a kill shot. He took that shot.

When he had the goods, the facts that caused indigestion in the Biden Whitehouse, Carlson didn't hesitate. He refused to water down devastating stories.

In July of 2023, Tucker Carlson gave an extended interview to podcaster Russell Brand. Carlson revealed that he had completed an interview with the man who served as the Chief of the Capitol Hill police during the January 6 events.

The man's name is Steven Sund, and he resigned shortly after the alleged insurrection.

Tucker explained that Steven Sund identified that the January 6 protester crowds were "filled with federal agents". Carlson bemoaned the fact that Fox fired him before the interview could be broadcast.

Fox News owns that Carlson interview with Steven Sund that has never seen the light of day, but Carlson is not afraid to talk about it.

In a strange way, because of this drive to expose the truth, Carlson emerged as more than a man who saved McCarthy and Trump. He was becoming an important figure himself, internationally.

McCarthy wasn't the target anymore. Trump wasn't the target anymore.

The emperor bragged about his fabulous new clothes: the

border, the economy, and the welfare of children and minorities. But yelling above the din was a brave little boy separating himself from the crowd. "The Emperor is naked!" yelled the lad. And the child's name was ...Tucker Carlson.

And Tucker Carlson was not being quiet or going away.

America's newest hero is becoming our nation's last best hope to stop the disintegration of free speech and end the corruption of American culture. He is fearless.

He is one Tough Mother Tucker.

Now with a target on his back.

CHAPTER 18
ANTI-CELEBRITY

Anyone who has not been living under a rock for the last 10 years or so knows that Tucker Carlson has truly reached the stratosphere of celebrity and fame.

His Fox news broadcasts at 8 PM Monday through Friday were the highest rated television program in that slot for years, even surpassing the big numbers generated by his predecessor in that hour, Bill O'Reilly.

Carlson's recent departure from the Fox News Channel has generated so much media buzz that Carlson's public profile has actually been enhanced. What this means is that even without his Fox News program, Carlson is now more famous than ever before.

And that makes Carlson even more interesting for one reason.

He doesn't act like a celebrity.

He doesn't travel with an entourage, and he doesn't have any bodyguards. He's interested in the simple pleasures of life like fishing and hunting with his buddies. And what he cherishes most is not the spotlight but rather the chance to be with his wife and children.

In other words, Tucker Carlson really is an authentic family man.

Most of the time, during his many years at Fox News, he would end the broadcast with his famous tagline in which he urged the viewers to "spend time with the ones you love."

So essentially, Tucker Carlson lives his life in a way that flies in the face of what you might otherwise expect from a highflying celebrity. In other words, the news commentator with whom America is most obsessed is in a word… normal.

Yes, many find it shocking but Tucker Carlson is amazingly and reliably normal. It's almost boring to think about how normal he is but to some extent it's not unexpected.

Tucker Carlson strives to keep his feet on the ground despite his great wealth and notoriety. He certainly has an ego but his is standard size especially when you compare him to all the other egomaniacs who populate the world of media celebrity.

Here are just a few examples and stories that demonstrate that Tucker Carlson behaves in a way that is more like your average Joe than your average Joe Namath.

Let's begin with his on-camera appearance.

He rarely buys a new wardrobe. Unlike the days when O'Reilly was provided brand-new suits from Hickey Freeman in return for a little TV promotion, Carlson eschews the idea that he should be adorned in the latest fashions.

If you've been watching carefully over the years, you will notice that just like the rest of us in the world, he has a few shirts and ties in his closet that he recycles over and over again about once every two weeks.

He has a favorite blue-and-white patterned shirt that reappears every several days. He also has a total of about 15 ties all of which are in the regular rotation for his television appearances.

He's got to be the only national television personality who dresses like an accountant going back and forth from the same office every day to put in his 8-to-10-hour shift. It's refreshing to see a TV personality who dresses like a regular guy instead of trying to be a fashion icon the way that Don Lemon used to for all of his CNN appearances before his contract was terminated.

The next topic is the famous Tucker Carlson hair.

It's strange that such a mundane thing would be such a topic of conversation on the Internet but on any given day you can Google "Tucker Carlson hair" and you will find a number of entries from a myriad of sources.

Here's the actual story.

Tucker Carlson has been blessed with a magnificent head of wavy light mahogany colored hair. If Tucker Carlson transitioned to become a woman and really let his hair grow out, he soon would be playing the role of Rapunzel in a Hollywood reenactment. The truth is that his hair is absolutely luxurious and it comes across so on camera.

It is so luxurious that various websites have conjectured with near certainty that Mr. Carlson is wearing a toupee. The theory that is going around is that nobody on television has hair that looks that good and looks that natural. Ergo, it must be a toupee.

It is not a toupee or wig but instead is the original hair with which he was blessed by the good Lord at birth.

In addition, Tucker Carlson not only has his own hair but he commits one of the great sins of Hollywood by having his hair cut at a barbershop instead of at one of the pricey salons used by California Governor Gavin Newsom.

The other thing about his hair is that Tucker frequently is too busy to remember to get it cut on a regular basis. As a result, Tucker's hair frequently becomes a little shaggy in need of a little trim or cut.

Interestingly, when he does forget to get his hair cut, it hair grows out and becomes even more luxurious as one wave of hair establishes an outcropping of a new wave. I know women that would kill to have his hair.

Another interesting quirk about his appearance has to do with his weight. It fluctuates on a regular basis. Tucker never looks fat or pudgy on television but you can see the way his jawline narrows when he is in one of his lighter weight phases.

One last quirk about the way he presents physically on television. He is genuinely interested in the topics he covers and is especially energized during his opening monologues when he tends to get excited especially when uncovering some fraud or charlatan. This is one of the things that draws viewers to his broadcast.

He is so genuine in his excited delivery that the viewer cannot help but share in the adrenaline rush. Millions of viewers feel that their day is incomplete until they've had a chance to enjoy the monologue of Tucker Carlson.

In any case, Tucker suffers from a weird quirk in which his salivary glands begin pumping with the same excitement that Tucker is feeling as he presents his monologue. As a result, Tucker has been known to spit or have a milky saliva paste accumulate on his lips or in the corner of his mouth.

It sounds gross but it really isn't as it adds to the excitement of the moment as America is tantalized by

Tucker's breathless revelations. By the time the camera operators go back to Tucker after the post monologue commercial break, the saliva has been wiped away and Tucker is ready to jump into his first interview.

The sum and substance of all this microanalysis of Tucker on camera is to say just one thing. He's just a normal guy trying to do good things never obsessed with his appearance.

This is so unlike the pretty boys and fashion models that serve as talking heads throughout the cable news industry. Tucker provides a contrasting dose of reality not only in the substance of his reports but in the way he projected himself into your living room Monday through Friday.

It would take days for you to examine all the video clips of Tucker Carlson available on the Internet. In fact, it might take weeks given the amount of television time he has had on air over the many years.

In addition, because Carlson does not travel with an entourage of bodyguards, you can find video snippets of Carlson on *YouTube* where average citizens encounter him living life.

One video that went viral truly demonstrated him as a normal guy and not some kind of elitist. Tucker is a real fisherman and he has a favorite location up in a little town called Livingston, Montana. He likes to go there with his friends and family, usually staying at some cheap motel while his group plies the waters for some beautiful fishing.

Not too far from the hotel is a hunting and fishing retail store where Tucker and his family like to go to stock up on supplies like ice, coolers, and fishing gear.

One day while waiting to pay the cashier at the supply store, a complete stranger got in Tucker's face and told him that he was the worst person in the world. The man was aggressive and it seemed like he was also potentially violent.

Tucker later explained on a radio podcast that he felt "rattled". He was especially troubled because his young daughter was with him and the entire situation made her feel uncomfortable and afraid. Tucker also found it pretty suspicious that some cohort of the aggressor happened to be making a video record of the entire encounter.

Maybe the bigmouth thought he was a hero with this video record as his trophy proving he confronted the TV host.

The whole incident only lasted a few seconds and Tucker just continued on with this trip never filing a police report or complaint. Tucker really is just a normal person trying to live his life unmolested and never seeking any additional publicity or promotion. He just wanted to go fishing and be left alone with his family and his friends.

Obviously the man that got in his face was simply a jerk but Carlson handled the situation with aplomb, just trying to diffuse the situation not of his own making. Just a normal guy.

Another great video demonstration of Tucker's averageness involves fishing again. Tucker Carlson discovered that authorities permit flyfishing in many of the ponds throughout Central Park in New York City. Leaving his New York City offices, fishing rod in hand, he parked himself in a serene spot on the edge of the water, looking for the largemouth bass that call Central Park their home. One day a social media video hound began confronting Carlson as he peacefully tried to catch a big one at Central Park.

The video available on *YouTube* shows that the cameraman was a little creepy as he snuck up behind Tucker. The two men have a brief conversation as Tucker explains that park authorities do indeed permit flyfishing in Central Park. Tucker asked him about his video practices but is not aggressive at all.

In fact, Tucker comes across as downright friendly, which is surprising because the videographer acted like he was producing some kind of exposé of the Fox news personality.

In the end, the videographer admits that Tucker was nice, patient, and reasonable especially since Carlson really was just seeking a few moments of private peace and serenity. Again, no police reports were filed, and Tucker Carlson continued on his merry way, America's number one political pundit normal guy.

How is it that the most high profile personality on television leads a life so lacking in celebrity and adulation?

There are essentially two reasons for this. The first one is Tucker's family. He stays very close to his wife and children and will not attend Hollywood parties or movie premieres or glitzy social gatherings.

Carlson is a homebody. He wants to do his job and then spend the rest of his time with his wife and kids. And this keeps him grounded. When you stay within the cocoon of your own nuclear family, it is impossible to become bigheaded because they don't care about your television ratings or your latest media appearance.

For Tucker Carlson the greatest title he has ever achieved is that of dad. He cherishes his wife Susie and is protective of his family to the point where he regularly says no to opportunities that other celebrities would jump at. He's happy where he is and with what he has achieved and is not looking for the next rung up on the media ladder.

Tucker and Susie Carlson, the ego-free power couple

The second reason for Tucker Carlson's somewhat diminished ego in comparison to his contemporaries has to do with the way he himself accesses media sources.

He doesn't do it.

Sounds weird, right?

Yes, it is downright weird but Tucker Carlson rarely accesses social media in any way whatsoever. He will on rare occasion create his own postings on different social media sites but he never himself reads or reviews social media outlets. He doesn't want to and so he doesn't.

He is truly at peace with himself, so he sees no benefit in seeing what anybody else has to say about him on *Facebook.* It takes real discipline to resist immersing oneself in the cacophony of social media noise. Tucker Carlson is a nonplayer and very happy to be sitting on the sidelines when it comes to social media. Currently, he is producing content on *Twitter*, but once it is posted he is done with it.

I have of course indicated that Tucker Carlson does not access media sources himself, but he takes this discipline even one step further beyond social media nonparticipation.

Tucker Carlson does not own a television.

Just in case you think this is a typo, let me repeat: *Tucker Carlson does not own a television.*

The man who has appeared before television cameras more than any other man on earth in the last 15 years does not own a television. This means that he never watches himself. He is constantly preparing and researching so that he is ready for the next broadcast, but he never gets bogged down in the microscopic self-analysis all too common for television stars.

This television star without a television is so self-effacing that he doesn't regard himself as a television star. This is unbelievable in an era where fame and self-promotion are the singular goals for those striving to make it in the fast-paced world of modern media communications.

Many media stars have committed career suicide because they let their egos get in the way of working hard and clean living that helped them achieve success in the first place.

Not Tucker Carlson.

The fact is that you may hate his politics and you may hate his programs. But if you have a clear perception of who he really is, you can't hate him.

If you lived next door to him and you asked him to help carry a couch out to the tree lawn so it could be picked up by the garbageman tomorrow morning, he'd immediately drop what he was doing and grab his end of the sofa.

A normal guy with extraordinary dedication to his craft rising to the occasion presenting truth to the American people.

That in a nutshell is Tucker Carlson, the anti-celebrity.

CHAPTER 19
WORST OF THE WORST

Tucker Carlson was once asked to identify the very worst person he had ever interviewed.

Carlson of course has interviewed likely upwards of a thousand different people throughout his storied career having found himself face-to-face with some of the truly notorious characters in government, business, arts, and entertainment.

Carlson has talked to murderers and corporate leaders who have placed corporate greed above public health and safety.

However, Tucker truly hates people who engage in personal self-promotion at the expense of normal everyday people just trying to survive.

Just a few years ago Carlson highlighted the career of the ultimate self-promoter willing to sacrifice anyone's career or business in an effort to enhance his public prominence. Carlson detailed the reasons why he reviled this man in an article he published in the *Weekly Standard* in 1995.

The man's name was John Banzhaf the Third and he

stands alone in Carlson's estimation in a very special place where ego intersects with mediocrity and lack of integrity.

John Banzhaf is a scam artist masquerading as a social justice warrior.

Banzhaf has a day job where he serves as a law professor at George Washington University in Washington DC.

However, he has become the king of trivial lawsuits only for the purpose of creating a false public impression that Banzhaf is for justice for the little guy.

The problem is that Banzhaf makes a practice of filing lawsuits against small business operators so that he can get his name out there as a lawyer attempting to rid society of its many ills.

Banzhaf found a way to pursue racial equity and the elimination of all forms of discrimination in a way that trivializes these causes and causes harm to small business operators trying to make their way in the world.

Carlson outlined a ridiculous lawsuit against a small dance studio for children. Banzhaf's litigation charged the operator with failure to create a racial balance in the tiny population of dance students. Poor Mrs. Simpson, the founder of the studio, was forced to spend thousands of dollars in attorney fees and eventually agreed to the mandatory appointment of monitors to oversee the implementation of new racially equitable recruitment procedures for the studio. Banzhaf created a small bureaucracy that turned a charming little dance group into a highly regulated project where the guidance from lawyers became more important than teaching little Jimmy the foxtrot.

Banzhaf was proud of what he did, but Carlson was disgusted. Mrs. Simpson suffered while Banzhaf gained fame as an attorney.

As modern society pursues casual attire eschewing the jacket and tie as the uniform of the day, dry cleaners have been going out of business by the thousands. It just got worse as people started working remotely in their homes, frequently interacting with coworkers by zoom. Getting work done while wearing pajamas in your living room meant even further reduction in the need for a dry cleaner for your suit or your dress.

These days, lots of men don't even own a tie or suit coat. The days of a dry cleaner on every corner are long gone and the dry cleaners that are left struggle to survive.

That's when the drycleaners became suitable prey for Banzhaf the publicity hound. He discovered that women's apparel could be dry cleaned but mostly at prices higher than the average comparable man's suit. For this reason, he went after the dry cleaners in Washington, most of which were individually owned family operations.

Banzhaf brought them to their knees in a sex discrimination lawsuit that forced the operators to alter their pricing structure. These tiny dry-cleaning shops were frequently operated by immigrants working 12 hour days six or seven days a week. Most Americans would be inspired by their work ethic and by their noble pursuit of the American dream.

Banzhaf saw them merely as an opportunity to pretend that he was eliminating a horrible injustice. Banzhaf treated them like pariahs instead of entrepreneurs sweating it out each day using hot steam irons to eliminate wrinkles in your favorite suit.

Banzhaf even turns himself into his own press agent as he never waits for media to contact him with a comment about his latest conquest. He is proactive in urging reporters to publish his comments about his latest victory.

He eventually turned himself into *McExpert*. Reporters publishing stories related to almost any form of litigation realized that Banzhaf was at the ready and available to offer an expert opinion always needed to put lawsuit stories into context.

Laziness inherent in human nature helped make Banzhaf a media star because getting a quote from Banzhaf was as simple as responding to Banzhaf's unsolicited emails and phone calls. One reporter admitted his laziness, using quotes from Banzhaf in 17 different articles covering a range of topics simply because Banzhaf made himself uber available.

Carlson probably wouldn't see Banzhaf as such a terrible person if Banzhaf pursued truly noble causes.

However, it seems that Banzhaf loved publicity so much that the stupid nature of the claim was no barrier to him initiating litigation.

As result, Banzhaf became a warrior to make sure that fancy restaurants couldn't be forced to make a man wear a suit coat. Good taste and dress code standards had to go in order to protect men from this unfair practice.

Banzhaf also crusaded against ladies' nights at bars and taverns. He could not tolerate the injustice of women getting free drinks while their male counterparts had to pay full price.

Banzhaf didn't care that tavern keepers increase their profits through the use of ladies' nights. Banzhaf realized that there must be sacrifices in the name of sexual justice.

Banzhaf also became the champion of something he called "potty parity" in which he forced establishments to equalize the number of toilets in the men's and ladies' rooms. God forbid that the men's bathroom should have a higher number of commodes than the ladies' room, even in establishments where the clientele was overwhelmingly male.

Banzhaf even went after the barbershops in the metropolitan area surrounding the District of Columbia. As result of his legal efforts, the disgusting situation in which ladies' haircuts were more expensive than men's has been stamped out. Praise the Lord that the universe has been saved because Banzhaf put a stop to this ultimate evil.

Even tough-minded barbershops cried uncle when targeted by "Banzhaf's Bandits".

Carlson also found it disgusting that Banzhaf frequently enlisted the help of his law students in pursuing these nonsense lawsuits. Most of the future lawyers in his classes enjoyed helping Banzhaf with the litigation because they found it interesting and entertaining. Carlson saw how disgusting it was that "Banzhaf's Bandits" were having quite a bit of fun at the expense of hard-working citizens.

Banzhaf told Carlson that his life's work fell under the noble heading of public interest law.

Carlson truly admired lawyers who took up unpopular causes where severe injustice demanded someone to come to the rescue. That's why Carlson frequently featured Harvard law professor Alan Dershowitz on his programs, because Dershowitz was willing to oppose mainstream opinion in favor of protecting constitutional rights.

Carlson found John Banzhaf to be a despicable self-promoter.

Banzhaf on the other hand, really was the worst person that Carlson had ever interviewed because he clearly cared only about his own personal publicity and was willing to destroy innocent people and their businesses in order to get it.

If you want to be famous, let that be an outgrowth of a noble pursuit. Carlson will praise you to the heavens if you strive to fight significant injustice.

But if you are John Banzhaf, he will expose you.

Frauds and hucksters, you have been warned.

CHAPTER 20
NO EGO

Even though Carlson was pegged as the heir apparent for Bill O'Reilly in the ever-important prime time 8 o'clock spot, there was one huge difference between Carlson and his predecessor that became very clear even after the first few weeks of Tucker Carlson in that important timeslot.

The difference was ego.

Bill O'Reilly had kind of a blustery dominating personality and was cocky during his broadcast, always maintaining a certain air of superiority.

Bill O'Reilly had a huge ego.

And he demonstrated that ego by making sure that even with friendly interview guests, it came across that all O'Reilly always had the upper hand in the conversation that he confidently controlled. Guests with superior knowledge and experience knew that it was important to refer to O'Reilly as the one with the superior intellect.

In other words, every interview and every story had to leave the viewer with the sense that the great and powerful O'Reilly had deigned to honor his audience with a display of his knowledge and righteousness. In some quarters at the Fox news Corporation, this made O'Reilly somewhat unbearable.

But O'Reilly was producing unbelievable numbers of viewers so much to the extent that some nicknamed him "the franchise". It was very much reminiscent of the old days at NBC when Johnny Carson's *Tonight Show* produced such a volume of advertising dollars that network executives dared not challenge the power of the late-night host.

And O'Reilly definitely was the Fox News Channel's cash cow. O'Reilly knew this and he flaunted it, frequently arrogant not just on the air but in his interactions with production staff.

For the Fox News Channel producers that stayed on to work on the *Tucker Carlson Tonight* program, the new host was a charming breath of fresh air who seemed to drink from the cup of humility every single day.

Tucker Carlson has given hundreds of interviews throughout his career and they are almost always marked by his self-deprecating view of himself. A typical interview with Carlson given to a print reporter or maybe even a small-market radio station begins with the interviewer thanking Carlson for the interview and complimenting Carlson and his fabulous success. In every instance, Carlson seems a little embarrassed, anxious to get to the substance of the interview and away from the fawning introductory remarks from the interviewer.

In other words, despite all his successes, Tucker Carlson really is humble, filled with the self-awareness that the great and mighty can come crashing down at any moment. Tucker Carlson strives to avoid the big headedness that frequently precedes the end of a great career.

In one of these interviews, Carlson attributes this lack of

ego to his father's advice. Richard Carlson was a very successful public figure who told his son Tucker to remind himself about the "jerk who lurks inside the heart of each one of us". Tucker Carlson never forgot about this advice although he did disclose that his father may have substituted a more colorful term for the word "jerk".

So when Tucker Carlson took over for Bill O'Reilly back in 2017, Carlson created a show different from the O'Reilly program because Carlson really wanted the broadcast to focus on the story and not on the host.

The idea that Tucker could serve as merely the conduit of truth as opposed to the Greek God of Truth quickly distinguished him from the bombastic Bill O'Reilly. Make no mistake, Carlson admired the way O'Reilly broke stories and exposed frauds. But it wasn't important to Carlson for each show to end with Carlson wearing the laurels of heroism in the fashion of O'Reilly. When O'Reilly fell from grace it was a painful fall from a very high pedestal constructed by O'Reilly himself.

Tucker Carlson would never build a pedestal for himself. He was satisfied to let others bask in the limelight while he merely served as ringmaster for an excellent production.

This is the reason why Tucker Carlson was always generous with his guests who benefited from a Tucker Carlson appearance. English writer Mark Steyn sold hundreds of thousands of books and became a popular host in his own right in the podcast world because of his many appearances as a commentator on the Carlson show.

In fact, Mark Steyn has appeared with Tucker Carlson more than 200 times on the *Tucker Carlson Tonight* production. This did not bother Tucker in the least. Tucker doled out these guest spots in a way that best served the program, even if the guest was getting rich from book sales and other opportunities. Tucker didn't care.

When protesters were tearing apart the City of Seattle and creating their own autonomous zones in promotion of social justice, Tucker discovered a Seattle radio talk show host by the name of Jason Rantz. Tucker was so impressed with Jason's reporting that he became a regular on the Tucker broadcast, appearing over 100 times on Tucker's nightly show. Again, Tucker's attitude was that there was plenty of glory enough to go around for everyone and that Jason Rantz's enhanced popularity was good for everybody.

Tucker liked you and put you on his show if you had talent and you were willing to tell the truth. Many thought it odd that Carlson put journalist Glenn Greenwald on the program. Greenwald was known as pretty liberal on most issues and well-known for his taking up the cause of classified document leaker Edward Snowden. Greenwald was dubbed by far-left commentator Rachel Maddow as "the American left's most fearless political commentator."

Again, none of this mattered to Tucker Carlson because Glenn Greenwald was willing to tell the truth and he ended up on the Carlson show on a regular basis. In fact, Greenwald became a reliable source for heretofore unknown facts related to Joe Biden's cozy relationship with Chinese and Ukrainian officials. Greenwald was officially punished by Rachel Maddow by being banned from further appearances on MSNBC.

This really didn't matter because Greenwald's frequent appearances with Tucker Carlson pushed Greenwald's book sales into the stratosphere. Before you knew it, Greenwald was selling millions of books and therefore accumulating independent wealth simply because Tucker Carlson valued dynamic truth tellers.

Tucker Carlson did not care if his guests were achieving success because these appearances made for a better show with more authentic truth that could not be found anywhere else.

The other thing about Tucker's generosity in handing out those precious guest slots was that Tucker Carlson truly wanted to do what he could to make this a better world when given the opportunity.

Because of this philosophy, Tucker was not above putting candidates on the air especially those aligned with Carlson's values of hard work, honesty, and American capitalism as a barrier against the creep of socialism in American politics.

Carlson was suspicious of politicians generally and only put candidates on the air that proved themselves to be true devotees of American exceptionalism.

For this reason he only allowed candidates airtime in those rare occasions when the candidate placed love of country above a desire to be part of America's hypocritical ruling class. This meant that Republicans and Democrats would be admired by Carlson on the air if they met his standard. Republican leaders hated that Carlson would occasionally embrace Democrats but they realized that this was part of the Tucker Carlson integrity.

Two recent examples of Carlson's admiration for Democrats are Tulsi Gabbard and Robert F. Kennedy Junior. Although Gabbard has since officially left the Democratic Party, Carlson embraced her energetic refutation of the ruling elites constantly dragging America into unnecessary military conflict.

Much more recently, Carlson's interview with Robert F.

Kennedy Jr. demonstrated the sincerity of Carlson's desire to elevate the truth even if it is colored blue instead of red. Kennedy's outspoken opposition to the lies of Joe Biden demonstrated that Carlson cared more about his country than his political party.

What is trying to be conveyed here is that Tucker Carlson was willing to use the power of his program to support politicians if Carlson sincerely believed that this would aid the cause of freedom. Republican and Democrat power was threatened by revelation of the truth of what was happening in our country. Carlson knew that Democratic and Republican leadership frequently worked together to maintain power used to maintain the ignorance of the average citizen.

That's why Tucker Carlson used the power of his program to almost single-handedly elect a new Republican Senator in the State of Ohio.

J.D. Vance was a former Air Force pilot, law school graduate, and author who emerged from the poverty of Appalachia to become a dynamic first-time politician running for the United States Senate in Ohio.

Carlson perceived the importance of maintaining the Ohio Senate seat in the Republican column. But that really wasn't important to him as much as supporting a fresh new candidate dedicated to fighting socialism and the destructive cultural programs of the far left. J.D. Vance opposed transsexualizing children and opposed the growth of big government.

So how did Carlson respond? Here's how.

Throughout the period of the campaign, Carlson gave J.D. Vance the exceptional soapbox of multiple appearances on his program. Vance appeared with Tucker Carlson almost 50 times during the 18 months preceding the Senate election in Ohio.

J.D. Vance was catapulted into the Senate through appearances with Tucker.

To some people in media, it was a shocking abuse of the airwaves. Tucker Carlson was serving as a one-man band beating the drum for Vance's election.

In the hands of another host, the Vance appearances would seem to be too much of an example of a host imposing his personal views in order to elect the candidate of his choice.

But Carlson handled the Vance interviews with delicacy, letting Vance make his own case and frequently throwing the candidate a curveball to test his nimbleness when challenged.

In fairness, Carlson made clear that Vance's opponent was welcome on the program as well. But the Democratic candidate knew he would be no match for the penetrating interrogatories coming from the experienced Carlson.

Vance won the election in no small measure because of the Carlson interviews.

But Carlson was sincere and he did not make this effort with many other candidates. Just as he was careful checking his own ego and careful in researching his topics, Carlson was careful in the way that he attempted to influence political outcomes.

It was obvious to all that Carlson cared about his country and wanted to stop it from careening off the rails into a fiery crash created by socialism, cultural disintegration, and by lying elitists comfortably sipping martinis and manipulating public opinion in order to increase their own power.

Clearly, Carlson's success in television had given him some power of his own. But Carlson was only willing to use it in ways that helped others and could lead to a better country for his family and future generations.

CHAPTER 21
CLYDE CRASH COP

W hen I was a kid one of my favorite cartoon shows was called Clyde Crashcup.

Clyde Crashcup was a special segment featured on all the various editions of the *Alvin Show* that were produced in the 1960s. While Alvin and the Chipmunks were the main feature, the Clyde Crashcup segment caught on in popularity. Clyde Crashcup was a weird scientist coming up with new inventions, usually of things that already existed. The result was always some kind of catastrophe.

Just a few years ago a radio-controlled aviation organization called the *Tri-City Radio Control Modelers* created a special award called the Clyde Crashcup award which is given to radio-controlled aviation specialists who persevered in their craft despite several crashes along the way. The 2023 winner was Guillermo Castaneda who earned the distinction because several of his crashes were of the spectacular variety.

This chapter shall serve as my official nomination of Tucker Carlson to be given the Clyde Crashcup award.

Let me put it this way. If Tucker Carlson pursues an

assignment that takes him to foreign lands, do not go with him.

Or if you do, buy lots of life insurance, especially the kind that pays double if you are victim of an accident or of a terrorist attack.

The point here is that when Tucker travels, danger goes with him.

Here is but one example of his several brushes with death.

Tucker is the real-life Clyde Crashcup, frequently surviving near disaster.

With the ashes of the twin towers still smoldering in Manhattan, President George W. Bush launched an offensive meant to root out forces of Al Qaeda and the Taliban who may have been responsible for the atrocities that killed over 3000 innocent American citizens on the date of September 11, 2001.

The intrepid Tucker Carlson's news nose was twitching. Tucker realized that a huge story was brewing in the Middle East where the winds of war would soon carry American bombers to avenge the cowardly acts of that fateful day.

As usual, Tucker Carlson was oblivious of the danger, especially because he wanted a front row seat in the coming conflict. He also realized that getting to the Middle East after the launch of Bush's offensive would be next to impossible.

He therefore decided to get a jump on things. He planned to travel into Afghanistan at the Khyber Pass through Pakistan and then hunker down until the war came directly to him so that he could begin reporting. The entire project was underwritten by *New York Magazine* excited that they had a man in the field getting out there into the war zone before the fighting began.

However, to get into Afghanistan you had the first travel to Pakistan. It's not like you had a wide array of airline choices like you're planning a vacation in Florida. The only airline available was *Pakistan International Airways* and he nervously booked a ticket.

After a long flight, Carlson arrived safely in Pakistan and that's where he hit a dead end. He spent several days there learning about the culture and interviewing the natives, gathering some pretty interesting stories.

Tucker wasn't the only one with this idea. Reporters, defense contractors, and adventure seekers all had the same idea. The problem was that the American government had anticipated these efforts and they didn't want a bunch of scribes, salesmen, and war tourists poking around the landscape that would soon be the target of American missiles. They didn't want people getting in the way and especially didn't want nonmilitary folk to get killed.

This made sense and after several failed attempts to cross the Afghanistan border, Tucker admitted this was futile and he prepared to fly home to the friendly confines of the good old USA.

That's when the real adventure started. Tucker's nighttime flight from Islamabad had a brief layover in Peshawar close to the Afghanistan border. The schedule required the pilot to travel to the United Arab Emirates for a stopover in Dubai. By this time, the American bombing missions were underway, and the pilot had to follow a new much longer flight path to give the American bombardier pilots a wide berth.

Carlson sensed there was something unusual about this

return flight that would hopefully end with a friendly greeting from his wife when he got back home. Tucker Carlson's Spidey sense had him tingling with some kind of instinctive understanding that things were going to get rough. The flight into Peshawar was fairly without incident although Tucker's nervousness was elevated when the *Pakistani International* aircrew began the flight with a prayer.

Did they know something?

Everybody on that flight had an uneasy feeling. The whole thing was made worse by the fact that the Pakistani government prohibited the use of alcohol even on their airlines.

Everywhere else in the world smoking on planes had long been prohibited but *Pakistani International Airlines* permitted smoking supposedly as some kind of concession to the idea that the alcohol prohibition created a special need to do something else to ease the tension.

As a result, the only beverage available was black coffee and you've never seen so much java consumed by a nervous group of people barely visible because of the thick blue cloud of cigarette smoke.

The scene was surreal as hard-boiled journalists and world travelers exchanged smokes and gulped gallons of bad-tasting joe served at room temperature. It's like they were all stuck in the world's worst diner except this airborne greasy spoon didn't have food.

It reminded everybody of that scene from Alfred Hitchcock's *The Birds* where a group of terrified citizens contemplated the danger lurking outside as they sat anxiously in a tiny café.

The flight made it safely to Peshawar airport and Tucker was relieved. The next leg of the trip would land in Dubai and from there Tucker would catch an international jet into New York City. He was getting close to being able to go home and he told himself to calm his nerves and stick it out.

Just before the plane took off for its Dubai destination, about 50 new passengers boarded the plane even though there were no seats available. The sense of danger heightened.

It's almost as though the new arrivals realized that this was their last chance to escape from hell. It was reminiscent of those scenes at the end of the Vietnam War where refugees from the communist onslaught would do anything to get on that last plane out of Saigon. They all knew what was coming and a place on that plane would likely be the difference between life and death.

In addition to the aisles crowded with passengers just boarded, Carlson noticed that the door to the cockpit remained wide open with a number of the extra passengers squatting on the floor between the pilot and the copilot. Carlson wondered if the plane was overloaded to the point where maybe it was too heavy for takeoff.

The pilot gently coaxed the plane into the air and soon thereafter the plane was cruising over the Arabian Sea.

Suddenly a loud bang thundered throughout the cabin, Carlson for a moment thinking that they had crashed into a building. He dismissed this thought because he knew the jet had been at cruising altitude.

Then the plane vibrated and entered into a steep drop. It seemed like this was it. The end.

Then miraculously, the plane straightened out but only halfway. The plane was moving in a basically horizontal fashion but was struggling to maintain this position.

It was almost as if something was tugging at the fuselage,

trying to drag it down into the watery depths of the Arabian Sea. Carlson and his seatmate, a war photographer from Croatia, were now nervously bathed in sweat.

The photographer stopped the flight steward who was rushing down the aisle, stepping between the extra passengers who also wore a look of terror. When the photographer asked the steward what was going on, the steward smiled and said that everything was fine.

It wasn't.

They were approaching Dubai airport and the pilot went in for the landing. The plane landed with a hard cracking sound but appeared to be in one piece as it jolted along the runway at a very high speed. It bounded off the runway into a sand dune but that did not slow it down very much.

The plane was in the middle of the landing from hell and the only real question was whether the cabin would be crushed with everyone inside. It was a nighttime landing and Carlson saw sparks flying off the right wing of the plane as it scraped against the ground.

All the electrical systems also failed so that the interior was bathed in darkness. The ill-fated plane finally came to a stop with the right side of the fuselage leaning against the tarmac.

However, the cabin was intact and everyone inside was alive!

That's when the next wave of terror hit the occupants. The cabin was filled increasingly with the smell of jet fuel and some kind of electrical odor. People were beginning to realize that they had to get out of that plane before it exploded.

The same flight steward yelled for everybody to remain in their seats. He explained that it was against the rules to exit the cabin before the pilot had given the signal that it was safe to disembark. Carlson ran to the front exit only to find it completely inoperable, likely fused closed from the heat generated by the crash landing.

Carlson decided to give the door one more try summoning all the superhuman effort that he could. It was a lucky thing that he did.

The door sprung open, and a huge inflatable slide instantly filled with air and one by one Carlson and the passengers rode that slide to *terra firma*.

Still anticipating an explosion, Carlson ran like a madman to put distance between himself and that hellish Pakistani International airplane.

The explosion never came but Carlson didn't care. He was alive!

Once again Carlson had defied the gods of international war travel.

Apparently, the gods of international war travel had been overruled by the Christian God who had big future plans for Tucker Carlson and the Fox news channel.

Clyde Crashcup had survived another episode!

CHAPTER 22
COVERT COVID OPERATION

Many years ago, with the Russian bear forcing complete control over European populations held prisoner behind the Iron Curtain, Americans struggled mightily to make sure that the true facts about the world made it to the ears of those poor people living under the communist boot.

That's when we invented something called *Radio Free Europe*. It's a private broadcast organization funded by the American government to penetrate communist countries with accurate information in an effort to give these imprisoned people hope that there's a better life outside the walls and barbed wire fences of the communist regime.

The fall of the Berlin Wall and the freedom movement initiated by Lech Walesa in Poland were partially the result of the courage found in European citizens learning the real truth of what was going on from *Radio Free Europe*.

With Vladimir Putin reconstructing the communist totalitarian regime under a new name, *Radio Free Europe* is as important as ever as Putin imprisons and murders dissenters even in this modern age.

Today one of the *Radio Free Europe* offshoots, *Radio Free Asia*, broadcasts to the people trapped inside the gulags of the Chinese and North Korean governments.

When it comes to the Covid crisis that overshadowed the world and almost destroyed American civilization, we had in America what became the important equivalent of *Radio Free Europe*.

That was Tucker Carlson.

The American government through its agencies and big tech collaborated with all the large pharmaceutical companies.

As we enter into this post-coronavirus era, the unbelievable magnitude of the lies perpetrated on the American people is beginning to emerge.

And no one would have access to the truth if we didn't have our own version of *Radio Free Europe* during the Covid years.

Without question Tucker Carlson had the biggest platform and the loudest megaphone as he courageously questioned government misinformation and published the raw data demonstrating one of the most insidious government conspiracies in the history of the world.

Here's what happened.

The discovery of the Covid virus presented an unprecedented opportunity for two big things to happen to benefit gigantic monolithic organizations.

The first was Big Pharma, the pharmaceutical industry. Ratcheting up public fear and mandating vaccines meant that Big Pharma was in for its biggest payday ever.

To pull this off, the government had to lie about the

efficacy of the vaccines and the government had to hide the data demonstrating the health dangers in getting the shot.

To add insult to injury, our government also created statutory immunity from civil liability for those harmed by this dangerous untested preventative inoculation.

And making things even worse, the government used your tax dollars to pay for these vaccines so that the pharmaceutical companies could grow in stratospheric wealth without having to convince doctors or citizens.

The government passed mandates and before you knew it your very livelihood was imperiled if you chose to be among that relatively small but knowledgeable minority unwilling to take the risk of this dicey injection.

The second big thing regarding the virus involved our government itself. Spreading fear and terrifying the population allowed the government to turn our citizens into zombie subservient cult members who would never do anything against the wishes of the cult leaders.

Americans voluntarily abandoned the right to attend churches and synagogues. We routinely cooperated in keeping children from school and even went along with the closure of restaurants and other small businesses.

Without firing a shot, the American government completed a *coup d'état* in which leaders drunk with power seized control of your daily lives and even of your minds.

Never in the history of the world had so much power been turned over to government leaders without the use of guns and bayonets.

Big tech was enlisted to play a major role in promoting lies and fear by censoring the facts and data disproving the government and Big Pharma narrative.

Independent physicians like the group known as the

Frontline Doctors held news conferences extolling the virtues of therapeutic medicines as a solution making the use of vaccines and the risk of those vaccines unnecessary.

Twitter, YouTube, Facebook, and *Google* swooped in like a tactical unit deleting the presence of the *Frontline* information from the Internet, a place where 98% of Americans got their information.

Experienced independent physicians all over America not only proclaimed the success of therapeutics such as hydroxychloroquine and Ivermectin but they also presented the raw data coming in from all over the world that demonstrated that the vaccine was essentially ineffective in stopping the spread.

But that didn't matter.

Truthful information had to be squelched so that American citizens would continue like lemmings running off the edge of a cliff by the millions because the warning signs as you approached that cliff were shrouded in censorship throughout the media world. *The New York Times, The Washington Post, and the Associated Press* joined forces with our internet masters to build an impenetrable wall around the truth.

The truth is that the vaccine itself was responsible for thousands of deaths without even being effective as a tool to create immunity. Eventually, we would be told to be quiet and instead to look at the vaccine as a way to diminish the severity of the Covid symptoms.

The truth, however, did force its way into the public consciousness. There were a few talk show hosts, especially on AM radio, who told the truth, and a few other small media outlets that tried to expose the dangers and the lies.

For the most part, this information lockdown was

working as the major broadcast networks followed the lead of big tech. So overbearing was the seek and destroy effort of big tech that publishing anything on *YouTube* or *Facebook* that even implied the ineffectiveness or the dangers of the vaccine meant that you would be deplatformed.

In other words, your effort to share accurate information with the world would be stopped dead in its tracks.

In fact, you faced the ignominious fate of being denied access to public platforms. This was the equivalent of the following: imagine the phone company listening in on your telephone conversations, then canceling your phone service because you said something they didn't like or that they didn't agree with.

Under the banner of stamping out misinformation, the concept of free speech had simply become a thing of the past in the country that invented the First Amendment.

But hold on.

The almost universal punishment for telling the truth about Covid, the ineffective and dangerous vaccines, and the destruction created by mask wearing and lockdowns was a punishment that would not deter Tucker Carlson.

While doctors and university professors cowered in their offices amidst piles of data exposing the truth, Tucker Carlson found scores of brave souls willing to tell Tucker's audiences what was really happening.

Among those brave experts was Dr. Scott Atlas who temporarily served as a coronavirus advisor for President Trump. He is a medical doctor educated at the University of Illinois Urbana and the University of Chicago. He is also a senior fellow at the Hoover institution at Stanford University.

As long as Atlas had the courage to appear, Carlson had the courage to let him identify specific data and specific studies proving the vaccine ineffective and proving the vaccine dangerous in many applications.

Dr. Marty Makary is a professor of medicine at John Hopkins University, and he stepped forward in front of the studio lights and cameras of the Tucker Carlson show to warn Americans of the permanent heart damage and life-changing injury emanating from a condition known as myocarditis.

The horror came from the vaccine causing major myocarditis events in young people and children who otherwise did not even need the vaccine. Studies demonstrated that youthfulness created a virtually impenetrable shield of protection against serious effects of the coronavirus.

Our government and Big Pharma were pushing the vaccine on people that didn't even need it and then looking the other way when these vaccine guinea pigs saw their lives ruined by permanent heart damage.

The major world information outlets were failing to keep the lid on the truth because Tucker Carlson kept hammering away even though sometimes he really felt like he was alone. However, the truth was leaking out more and more as he continued to bravely and authentically speak truth to power.

Tucker Carlson was the only significant media outlet to publish reports from the *Israeli Health Ministry* demonstrating a huge spike in myocarditis in the young males who had received the vaccination.

Tucker repeated the brave protests of Dr. Peter Liu who was the chief scientific officer at the University of Ottawa Heart Institute. Liu was alarmed at the incidence of myocarditis among the young caused by the vaccine. Dr. Liu's statement couldn't be found anywhere else because *Google was deleting its presence* wherever it popped up.

And if you tried to repost these Carlson broadcasts on *Facebook*, *Twitter* or *YouTube*, the communist-like monitors swooped in to eliminate the post and punish the posters through techniques like shadow banning, demonetization, and even deplatforming.

With a simple click of a mouse you could disappear from the digital face of the earth if you sought to offer information inconsistent with the government's Big Pharma viewpoint.

But Tucker Carlson trudged onward regardless of the lies perpetrated in other forums.

Tucker Carlson of course was but one voice frequently drowned out by the lies of the rest of the media world. But he was a voice that people were paying attention to because of the millions of followers dedicated to his weeknight program.

It is not an exaggeration to say without the truth telling by Tucker Carlson, the world would be mostly unaware of the lies given to us by the government and Big Pharma on the subject of Covid.

In many quarters, Dr. Fauci is now regarded as a slimy lying bureaucrat. Without Carlson, the vile misinformation parade would still be marching down Main Street in America.

Which leads us to perhaps the most significant way in which the presence of Tucker Carlson forced Americans to confront the insidious evil within our own government.

This involves the leak of the virus from the Wuhan Lab in China.

The story begins with Dr. Anthony Fauci's desire to initiate investigation of potential gain of function (viral migration from animals to humans) possibilities in various forms of the SARS virus many years ago.

Eventually, our government was spending millions of

dollars to understand how animal-based coronavirus could migrate to human hosts.

Fauci, realizing the controversial nature of this kind of experiment, decides to ship the experiments offshore to the Wuhan Lab in China which was under the direct control of the Chinese Communist Party.

Due to unprofessional scientific practices in the Wuhan Lab, the often-fatal virus does

Dr. Fauci strikes a noble pose: Carlson exposed his lies.

indeed find a human host in the various persons working at the lab. Before you know it, those people are circulating throughout the Chinese population and the Covid crisis is quickly in its infant stage within communist China.

It didn't take long for the aggressive virus to continue mutating and transmitting itself throughout populations, eventually landing on American shores.

Throughout the world, fear gripped everyone as millions died from the virus destroying the respiratory systems of its victims.

Emails between Fauci and his underlings show that Fauci tried to paper over his own responsibility for creating this monstrous pandemic.

Fauci and the World Health Organization with the encouragement of the Chinese Communist Party, circulated the idea that the virus originated from animal wet markets in China.

Despite this, several scientific and government studies demonstrated that the Fauci financed Wuhan Lab was responsible for the virus and its distribution throughout the world.

What a story!

And who was the only one willing to publish these facts?

None other than Tucker Carlson.

The major broadcast networks and the usual big tech suspects circled the wagons to refute Tucker's revelations.

Again, without Tucker at the microphone, very few of us even hear about this dramatic tale.

As the calendar turned into the year 2023, internal documents reflecting investigations conducted by various American agencies including the FBI showed one thing to be true: Tucker Carlson was right about the lab leak. The Chinese government and Anthony Fauci were complicit in the creation of the virus and in covering up its source in the Wuhan laboratory.

On the subject of Covid, Carlson towers above the media competition when it comes to telling the truth. In fact, Carlson's broadcast actions in providing a lineup of doctors, scientists, and investigative reporters who had the truth in hand was truly heroic.

Woodward and Bernstein showed an awful lot of moxie in exposing the machinations of Richard Nixon.

But they never showed the courage that Carlson displayed because Carlson was up against billion-dollar corporations and the full force of the federal government and the Chinese Communist Party.

Carlson was now taking his place in the pantheon of journalistic leaders such as Ernie Pyle during World War II and Edward R. Murrow in the late 1950s. Future students of journalism should study his programs and methods while the rest of us thank him for his tenacious dedication to the truth.

CHAPTER 23
MONICA LEWINSKY

To this very day the Monica Lewinsky scandal is referred to as the mother of all scandals.

After all, this scandal had everything that a news reporter could dream of. First of all, it involved the leader of the free world, the occupant of the most powerful office in the universe, the Presidency of the United States.

Secondly, it had that feature that gives zip and zing to any story in which it might possibly be found: sex.

It was a dream formula for selling newspapers and advertising time. The married President of the United States has a fling with a lonely female intern in the Oval Office at 1600 Pennsylvania Avenue and the sexual activities are even a little bit kinky.

For this reason, the Bill Clinton-Monica Lewinsky affair for almost 12 months straight was more responsible for a huge spike in periodical sales and television news viewership than during any other similar period of time in the history of the world.

In fact, there are media observers who feel that cable

television news, which unlike broadcast news didn't have to be sandwiched in between regularly scheduled programs, finally found its footing because of the eyeballs so tantalized by this story where power and eroticism converged.

Not since the O.J. Simpson murder trial had media encountered such a mother lode of solid gold storytelling. And it was all true!

As a result, every little piece of new detail, no matter how insignificant, became an urgent news alert subject to a breathless report from an excited television correspondent.

Everyone in media found a way to create their own take on the story so that the entire media industry could cash in on the story.

And if you could discover or create a new angle on the story or find some piece of information even on the fringes of the story, you had a way to attract the public's attention.

The muckrakers in the early 1900s perfected the concept of yellow journalism by making up stories out of whole cloth. It was pretty tough being a public figure back in those days when a scribe anxious to sell papers might randomly include your name in a story about prostitutes or serial murderers just for the heck of it because your name was well known and would drive up sales.

As the libel and slander laws became more sophisticated and journalists and publishers were held accountable, scandals had to actually be true in order to find their way into print.

That's why the Bill Clinton-Monica Lewinsky affair was such an incredible event. As scandals go it was bizarre, and sexy, and also true.

So Tucker Carlson the writer did his duty and wrote story after story, mostly rehashing known events. As a talking head, however, the story gave him multiple opportunities for speculation and pontification and along with his associates in cable news. Carlson racked up many hours examining the implication of the blue dress and Cuban cigars as sex toys.

Remarkably, Tucker Carlson himself got caught up in two separate Monica Lewinsky events in one case because of bad luck and in the other case because a related story landed in his lap.

Let's begin with the bad luck story. During that lengthy period of time when the Lewinsky story was constantly at the top of the news, Carlson got a phone call from an English reporter who was well-known for getting bombed night after night at various bars and taverns around the world.

This was his great reportage technique. He loved to drink, and he loved to talk and he did both with anyone and everyone who might stumble into the adult beverage establishment where he was hanging out.

Once he got someone talking, he would direct the conversation toward interesting topics. Remember, both the reporter and the interviewee are drinking heavily. In any case, this London reporter frequently stumbled home with a notebook full of amazing stories that could feature incredibly eye-catching headlines.

The only problem with this way of collecting information is that most of the stories turned out not to be true, owing to the fact that the witness was blind drunk telling the reporter things that he wanted to hear so that he could satisfy his supervisors at the news desk. As result, this reporter had a terrible reputation for concocting fake stories pretending to be a real truth seeker.

Things got so bad that it was rumored that the reporter

would soon be losing his job. It seemed that one too many fictional accounts had been reported as fact under his byline.

Back to the phone call from the dishonest reporter from across the pond. The English writer asked Carlson a few innocent questions related to his opinion of the Monica Lewinsky story and some of its featured details. The conversation was brief as Tucker obliged him, thinking that the reporter was truly interested in Carlson's opinion as perhaps a way of seeing the story through the eyes of a prominent American political pundit.

Carlson put the phone down and thought nothing further.

A week later, all hell broke loose. A major story about Bill Clinton and Monica Lewinsky appeared in the *Daily Mirror*, one of the biggest daily newspapers in the British Isles. The story was lengthy and was filled with salacious details describing sexual practices of President Clinton. Hundreds of words in that story were dedicated to Clinton's fetishes and preferences, the story reading more like an X-rated novel than a major feature in the British press. The story built to a crescendo of speculation on the future of the President from Little Rock, given the sex scenes described in the story's narrative.

It was something quite shocking.

Even in America, such titillating facts rarely made it into a story about the President. Carlson wasn't even sure it could be called journalism. It was closer to pornography.

And this is the most shocking part. The story was written by Tucker Carlson.

Or at least it was Tucker Carlson's byline included with the story in the *Daily Mirror*.

Carlson was inundated with phone calls from friends and associates surprised to see that Carlson was writing garbage regarding the Lewinsky matter for a British newspaper.

Carlson was enraged.

It did not take long for him to put two and two together and to realize the infamously drunken English reporter had developed a new technique: Conduct a brief telephone interview with a famous American pundit and then publish an erotic tabloid story under the pundit's byline.

If the English scribe were caught, he could say that Carlson directed the story by telephone because the phone records would show that the two parties had indeed communicated in a long-distance phone call.

But this was beyond anything Carlson had experienced in the world of reporting before.

On one prior occasion, he actually had a major American newspaper print Carlson stories under someone else's byline without his permission. In that case, Tucker did not even know how the newspaper had gotten hold of Tucker Carlson's copy. In fact, the thieving periodical had stolen the story before Carlson was finished with it and before Carlson could turn it into the magazine that had commissioned him to do the story to begin with.

But this was a horse of a different color completely. The *Daily Mirror* wasn't stealing a Carlson story: it was fabricating a Carlson story hoping to attract readers because of the Tucker Carlson name. And to add insult to injury the story was trashy and not written with the flare typical of a Tucker Carlson project.

There was nothing Carlson could do but grin and bear it. The laws in England are much more lax than in America and taking action against the *Daily Mirror* would've been a major distraction. Various other English newspapers picked up the story and reprinted it so copies of the story could be obtained anywhere in the British empire.

Carlson finally had a brief conversation with the publisher of one of the papers that did the reprint, but it was very unsatisfying. The young lady on the other end of the phone was rather blasé about the whole thing. Apparently, journalistic ethics just don't exist over there. God save the King.

The second major intersection between Tucker Carlson and the Monica Lewinsky story involved a situation where Tucker Carlson was gathering his own research about a previously unknown aspect of the young intern's life.

Carlson received a tip that Monica Lewinsky had several sex therapy sessions while a high school student in Beverly Hills, California.

This was a really weird tip and ordinarily Carlson would never follow up on such a thing, but he also knew that anything Lewinsky related could become a hot story.

So Carlson followed up by trying to track down this mysterious sex therapist. Carlson left a voicemail on the answering machine for a sex therapist named Irene Kassorla.

She called Carlson back from an Italian restaurant in Hollywood where she was enjoying a casual meal. She confirmed the story with Carlson but only in vague general terms.

Carlson was very skeptical and unlike his British counterparts in London, he was unwilling to run with such a story unless he had hard provable facts.

Carlson decided to dig deeper and see if this woman was truly a sex therapist or maybe just some kind of a nut job looking for her 15 minutes of fame.

The research was quite revealing. It turns out that

Kassorla was in fact a certified licensed sex therapist famous for writing sex manuals. She published her first in 1980 in the form of a book called *Nice Girls Do*. Carlson got hold of the book and discovered it to be more like a how-to article in *Cosmopolitan* instead of some kind of academic prose written by a professional.

The book, Carlson discovered, had become somewhat of a minor sensation, selling lots of copies mostly to lonely women looking for imaginary excitement. I guess you could say it was a precursor to the book *Fifty Shades of Grey* that reached great popularity around the year 2010.

Carlson thought the book and Dr. Kassorla herself were nonsense but that one unbelievable fact was absolutely true: Monica Lewinsky's parents paid for Monica to see a sex therapist while in high school.

Carlson couldn't figure out who was more disgusting, the therapist who provided sex therapy for a high school student or parents that would willingly pay for such therapy.

Poor Monica.

She never stood a chance.

How could an innocent young intern survive the oversexed libido of the President of the United States when Monica herself was probably all screwed up because of the nutty sex therapist?

Carlson however, was true blue to his calling as a reporter. He didn't want to hurt Lewinsky, but he knew that this story related to the sex therapist was floating out there in the ether and that some reporter somewhere, probably someone less responsible than himself, was going to run the story.

Carlson therefore was obligated to publish his findings in a story that appeared in the *Washington Examiner* in March of 1998. You can tell by reading the story that Carlson has

Tucker Carlson treated Monica Lewinsky with grace and sympathy.

nothing but contempt for the therapist and mostly sympathy for Monica Lewinsky.

The story is told tactfully and in a way that you can tell who the real villains are.

The story caused immediate ripples throughout the country and Carlson was hailed as a real newshound.

But I think from reading between the lines of the story, you can tell that Carlson feels a slight tinge of regret. But he is also pleased that he exposed the bizarre behavior of this supposed professional and Monica's parents.

Special prosecutor Ken Starr sent a subpoena to Kassorla and other stories about her circulated throughout the media and entertainment world. For a brief period of time, Kassorla saw a spike in her celebrity reminiscent of the post-publication days after her first sex book became a hit.

And that's how the Lewinsky story intersected with the life of Tucker Carlson. One story was completely fake and the second story demonstrated how a hard-boiled news man recognized the human vulnerability of a young girl at the center of the biggest scandal of the century.

Tucker Carlson carried forward with his career as the Lewinsky matter slowly faded away.

Tucker had bigger things ahead for him in the future and he hoped he would come across stories that were more meaningful and more substantive.

CHAPTER 24
SIMON SAYS

Former Catholic preacher father John Corapi used to talk about his love for little old ladies who had reached that advanced stage in life where they could say anything they wanted because their elevated age meant that they just didn't give a damn. In other words, they could speak the truth out loud regardless of the consequences because they were so old that nobody else could do anything about it no matter how much they objected.

This next chapter is a true exposition of Tucker Carlson's ardent love of truth as the theme of his very existence to the point where speaking anything other than the truth is completely foreign to him. There may be consequences to speaking the truth, but it means so much to him that when it comes to the consequences, he just doesn't give a damn. Here's the story.

Tucker Carlson published a new book in 2021 in conjunction with his publisher *Simon & Schuster*, perhaps one of the most powerful and distinguished publishers in the literary world.

The book was titled *The Long Slide* and like most releases these days, the book contains some introductory remarks related to the publisher itself. Authors use this as an opportunity to thank the publisher for the way they have helped the author in the editing, design, and promotion of the book. It's also a very smart thing to do to forge a good relationship with the publisher just in case future publications are contemplated.

Therefore, for obvious reasons, the author's introduction is frequently a love poem praising all the fabulous attributes of the brilliant publisher who has made it possible for the humble author to have his work distributed to the masses.

For this new book by Tucker Carlson, *The Long Slide*, the exact opposite was true.

In fact, Tucker Carlson actually made publishing history by attacking the president of *Simon & Schuster* in the opening pages of Carlson's new book published by *Simon & Schuster*. This is unbelievable.

Here's what happened. Tucker Carlson had finalized the terms of his publishing deal with the legendary house of *Simon and Schuster*. Carlson was just finalizing the manuscript when he noticed something strange.

United States Senator Josh Hawley, one of the more sophisticated and clearly more conservative of the Republicans in the Senate, had himself finalized a lucrative book deal with *Simon & Schuster*.

Hawley was renowned as a critic of Democrat party politics and *Simon & Schuster* knew exactly what they were getting when they agreed to publish Hawley's new book which was titled *The Tyranny of Big Tech*. Senator Holly's text was essentially an unmasking of the way that *Google, YouTube, and Facebook* were censoring conservative viewpoints and blocking content that might hurt Democrat politicians. *Simon & Schuster* saw this when they read the galleys and Senator Hawley's conservative agenda was clear from the get-go.

Then something strange happened. From the Senate floor, Senator Hawley called for a pause in the counting of electoral college votes out of concern for the possibility of irregularities in the 2020 election for president.

Simon & Schuster then canceled their book contract with Senator Hawley because he voted for this pause. It was completely ridiculous especially because Democrat senators had voted for an electoral vote count pause in the presidential elections of 2002 and 2016 because of concerns that Democrats had related to those elections.

Carlson got wind of the fact that *Simon & Schuster* had canceled Senator Hawley's book deal. Carlson then called the President of *Simon & Schuster,* Jonathan Karp, and confronted him. Karp admitted that the book deal was canceled at the request of Democratic politicians.

Carlson was outraged that a venerable publishing house like *Simon & Schuster* had allowed itself to be manipulated for political gain. Most disgustingly, *Simon & Schuster* was censoring a writer because they did not like the writer's politics. Carlson had become deeply concerned that our country was beginning to look more like the old Soviet Union as opposed to the First Amendment loving USA.

For this reason, Carlson launched a counterattack through the words that he used in the acknowledgement to the book he was about to publish with *Simon & Schuster.*

Here are the words found in the initial pages of the Carlson book:

I'd like to acknowledge Jonathan Karp of *Simon & Schuster* whose descent from open minded book editor to cartoonish corporate censor mirrors the decline of America itself. It's been a sad education watching it happen.

Those 35 words written by Carlson at the opening of his best-selling book were a shot heard round the world. Tucker Carlson was calling the Chief Executive Officer of his own publisher a "cartoonish corporate censor" and he was doing the name-calling in the very same publication distributed by his own publisher.

This was a truly remarkable event because it set a new standard in bold ballsy integrity. It is truly a miracle that *Simon & Schuster* continued with the publication of Carlson's book but it's also a testament to Carlson's power in today's media.

The most powerful man in the most powerful publishing entity in the world was willing to endure the humiliation of a

Senator Josh Hawley found Carlson defending him against a publisher.

scorching attack against himself and that most powerful man was the publisher of the attack.

Nothing like that before or since has ever occurred and it is not likely that it will ever occur again. Back in the 1940s and 1950s, MGM was run by the ironfisted Louis B. Mayer. There's no way Louis B. Mayer would authorize the production of a film that criticized Louis B. Mayer.

In this attack, Carlson was not just biting the hand that

feeds him, he was attempting to cut off the left arm that was feeding him.

Classic Tucker Carlson, and by the same token, typical Tucker Carlson. Did anyone in America have more testicular fortitude than Tucker Carlson?

I think not.

CHAPTER 25
DANCES WITH RUSSIAN BEARS

This next chapter is going to seem out of place like the events it describes seem completely out of place in the life of Tucker Carlson.

The only explanation I can offer for the contents of this chapter is that it is consistent with Tucker's willingness to put himself in harm's way in pursuit of an experience. Carlson will do almost anything to penetrate the depths of an exciting and important story.

It turns out that he'll even risk embarrassment if it means he can test himself with something new in the form of an unusual challenge.

Here's what happened.

The ABC television network had stumbled onto an unusual hit show called *Dancing with the Stars*. The program featured 12 professional dancers each of whom would be teamed up with a celebrity non-dancer in a competition where a celebrity would be eliminated each week until the last celebrity standing was crowned champion.

The celebrity contestants were drawn from many different categories of notoriety from sports to television to politics.

Tucker Carlson as a celebrity contestant was a somewhat unusual choice but still consistent with the network's desire to surprise audiences with celebrities that were bound to be perceived as a "fish out of water".

It was such an unusual choice that it really piqued audience interest to see a political pundit trying to prove himself on the dance floor. This kind of choice was so successful in attracting audiences that President Trump's press secretary Sean Spicer and Texas Governor Rick Perry also became part of the lineup in future seasons.

When asked why he accepted the invitation to appear on the dance program, Carlson explained that he was always looking for ways to challenge himself by engaging in activities for which he had little talent.

Audiences were interested in his participation when he was assigned Elena Grinenko as his professional partner and instructor. Grinenko had become famous after establishing a dancing career in Russia. With her Muscovite accent, Grinenko was Russian to the core. Viewers were curious to see how the famously anti-Russian conservative Carlson would get along with his dance partner from Europe.

Also intriguing was the contrast between the professional and the student in attitude. Tucker Carlson was known as a very reserved Episcopalian who embraced modesty as a virtue. It was a little bracing to seek Carlson in the studio twirling the scantily clad Grinenko engaging in provocative moves. Carlson, known famously as a faithful husband and family man, seemed uncomfortable opposite the sequined saucy Soviet.

America was fascinated by the unusual combination and

ratings for the program during Carlson's appearance were through the roof.

Unfortunately, the three professional judges gave Carlson some of the lowest scores in the history of the program and Carlson was eliminated in week one.

There are some pretty good reasons for his early departure.

First of all, Carlson's dance performance began with him sitting in a chair for the first 30 seconds of the routine. The idea was to have Carlson portray an innocent and naïve customer in a café who is hypnotized by the beauty that dances around him in a seductive effort to get him to dance with her.

It wasn't a bad plan for the dance because it really did tell a story. It was very similar to that scene in *American in Paris* were Gene Kelly portrays a greenhorn overcome by the sensual siren who invites him to dance.

Unfortunately for Tucker Carlson, he was no Gene Kelly. The Dancing with the Stars judges were also put off by Carlson remaining seated for such a long period of time. After all, intoned one of the judges, the program was supposed to feature dancing instead of sitting.

It was later learned that Carlson had been placed at a terrible disadvantage in this program. He had been assigned to cover a big story in Lebanon and he did so during the two weeks just prior to his dancing

Carlson danced with Grinenko, the Beauty from Moscow whose talents couldn't rescue him from early elimination.

debut. Carlson's celebrity competitors were practicing day and night while Tucker was somewhere in the Middle East. He just couldn't put in the preparation and practice needed to make a good showing.

It was obvious to all however that Tucker Carlson was a good sport and that he indeed had a good working relationship with the Russian professional.

When each of the judges announced the low scores for Carlson, the audience booed loudly. Carlson had won them over with his positive attitude and pluck. In the middle of Hollywood, this stalwart conservative had won the hearts of the likely liberal audience with his charm and graceful smile.

As the contestant eliminated first, Tucker Carlson finished in last place in season three of Dancing with the Stars.

He had scored a victory however.

Audiences that did not want to like him because of his politics, found themselves liking him because of his graceful happy warrior outlook.

Tucker Carlson loved the experience.

The Dancing with the Stars appearance just became one more positive building block in the reputation of Tucker Carlson.

CHAPTER 26
SMASHING THE KRISTOL BALL

What happens when the teacher becomes the enemy of the student?

The results can sometimes be jarring even though it doesn't happen very often. A great example from the world of sports involved Super Bowl champion quarterback Tom Brady when he left the New England Patriots to play quarterback for the Tampa Bay Buccaneers. Brady had spent his entire professional career under the tutelage of domineering football coach Bill Belichick and Brady had been an outstanding student. The Belichick-Brady combination produced five Super Bowl titles and nine conference championships.

Still, it was strange when the Patriots had to play the Tampa Bay Buccaneers for the first time after Brady's departure. It was now time for Belichick the teacher to defeat his favorite former student, Tom Brady.

The whole situation was weird because Brady had learned so much from the Patriots coach and now here he was doing battle with him. Patriots tight end Julian Edelman said it was like attending a family barbecue after a divorce with the two divorced parents attending for the sake of their child.

That's the weirdness that developed watching the relationship between Bill Kristol and Tucker Carlson disintegrate.

It's a pretty straightforward story but nonetheless interesting because of the personality of our two protagonists.

Tucker Carlson was still a wet-behind-the-ears journalist/columnist when he got the opportunity to leave his first job writing for the Arkansas Gazette, a relatively small newspaper.

His subsequent job was a lot closer to the big time. Bill Kristol had formed a powerful conservative commentary magazine, *The Weekly Standard*, which was financed by the famously conservative Rupert Murdoch.

Before you knew it, Tucker Carlson emerged as a star among conservative writers, using his trademark witty style to illuminate traditional conservative talking points related to all subjects under the sun.

Carlson was able to get this job because he had impressed *The Weekly Standard*'s founder, Bill Kristol. Kristol looked upon Carlson as his protégé, almost the same way proud a dad looks upon his talented son learning from the master and preparing to take over the family business.

Unfortunately for Kristol and *The Weekly Standard*, Carlson's pithy writing and aggressive debate style caught the attention of television producers seeking a dynamic foil to engage in verbal battle with liberal TV personalities.

Carlson always had a snappy retort for his liberal television opponents and before you knew it Carlson became the designated conservative on various television news programs.

Tucker Carlson of this era was right out of central casting, always wearing a bowtie and a button-down shirt that seemed the perfect uniform for the well-bred Ivy League style institutional conservative.

Bill Kristol saw Carlson grow into this TV role and he was proud the way a minor-league manager is proud to see one of his trainees get called up to the big leagues.

Everything was beautiful in the relationship between teacher and student.

The wheels came off the cart of that relationship right about the same time that Carlson realized that the elite ruling class he had been defending was lying to him.

The key event was Carlson's several weeks in Iraq where he saw firsthand that our government's nation building project was merely an excuse to keep the military-industrial complex in the money. American intervention in Iraq was a complete failure and George W. Bush was lying with the aid of elitist Republicans like Bill Kristol.

Carlson wrote about his disillusionment in the column he penned shortly after his return from Iraq.

Carlson was changed forever and vowed never again to be involved in a farce like that which had been cooked up by the ruling class as a justification for a brutal war.

From that point forward, Carlson had moved on and was a new and different man and a new and different kind of writer.

In the meantime, Bill Kristol and *The Weekly Standard* continued to back the intervention in Iraq and continued to support any other lie presented by elitist leadership in both parties.

After Carlson took over the 8 o'clock show from Bill

O'Reilly, the new always-tell-the-truth Tucker Carlson was unveiled for the world to see.

The old bowtie had been mothballed long before the *Tucker Carlson Tonight* show debuted on Fox News. But it wasn't long before Bill Kristol realized that Tucker Carlson was no longer drinking the Kool-Aid. Kristol understood that his once obedient apprentice was now an enemy tearing down the façade that Kristol and his country club friends had spent so much time constructing.

Bill Kristol was a great teacher but couldn't handle Tucker's success or his honesty.

The war was on. But since Kristol could not use truth as a weapon, Carlson being the one who saw the truth clearly and reported it, Kristol was reduced to attacking his former student with vile epithets.

Kristol told CNBC that the new Carlson program was "close to racism" and said that Carlson's monologues were "a combination of dumbing down... stirring people's emotions in a very unhealthy way".

Tucker Carlson's television ratings climbed into the stratosphere as he fearlessly spoke the truth regardless of the consequences.

As Carlson's star was rising, Bill Kristol's star was slowly plunging into the ocean of anonymity. *The Weekly Standard* shuttered its doors in 2018, partly because Kristol could no longer publish elitist BS in the face of revelations made on the *Tucker Carlson Tonight* TV program. Carlson had destroyed Kristol's credibility.

The bitterness from Bill Kristol really came out after an especially effective segment on Carlson's show in which Carlson demonstrated the idiocy of tearing down statues of our founding fathers all across the country. Carlson told viewers that George Washington's leadership both militarily and politically far overshadowed his ownership of slaves that was typical in the colonies of the late 1700s. Carlson said that slavery was wrong but not uncommon in the context of the times. Destroying statues was not an appropriate response in the modern age when the heroic leadership and humility of General Washington should be honored.

Bill Kristol reacted to the Carlson piece immediately and accused Tucker of "rationalizing slavery".

Tucker hit back hard by saying that Kristol no longer had an outlet for rational discussion since *The Weekly Standard* folded its tents in 2018. Carlson said that Bill Kristol has been reduced to firing off ill-conceived statements on *Twitter.* Said Carlson:

> *"At an age when he could be playing with his grandchildren, Kristol is glued to social media like a slot machine junkie in Reno. And after a while, of course, that distorts you."*

Carlson achieved further revenge against Kristol by featuring a caricature of Kristol on the front cover of Carlson's number one selling book *Ship Of Fools.* The drawing on the book cover portrays the fools who are helping to steer the ship of state of America, prominently featuring Kristol as one of those fools.

In an almost poignant closing remark in Carlson's response to Kristol's racism accusation, Carlson admits on camera that at one point in his life he genuinely liked Bill Kristol and thought that Bill Kristol liked him.

Obviously, the friendship between the two men was now over, Carlson victorious in his domination of mass media even after he left Fox News. In the meantime, Bill Kristol comes across like a bitter old man imprisoned by his inability to stop Carlson from exposing his lies.

This is a pretty sad story about two men whose friendship was sacrificed on the field of political opposition. But the truth is that Carlson never took direct aim at his old friend Bill Kristol until Kristol started publicly attacking Carlson's Fox News program. Carlson would've been perfectly willing to leave his old friend's name out of the discussion out of respect for his old boss.

Unfortunately, Kristol did not care about their relationship and certainly did not care about the truth, calling his old pal a racist when he knew that the exact opposite was true.

Sometimes you never really know who your friends are until you're the host of a national news program. I know this much: Tucker Carlson sleeps soundly at night but Bill Kristol is restless wallowing in lies hurtful to his former student, filled with rage. Truth has given Carlson celebrity and wealth, while deception has destroyed Bill Kristol's career. Bill Kristol will remain an overlooked footnote in media history.

CHAPTER 27
WILD AND CRAZY GUY

Back in the 1980s comedian Steve Martin developed a character who appeared in multiple skits along with Dan Aykroyd. They played the role of a couple of young male immigrants from Europe on the make in search of female companionship.

The bit was hilarious especially when Martin described himself, using a strange Eastern European accent, as "a wild and crazy guy".

As Steve Martin played tour dates throughout America, he reproduced the character of the wild and crazy guy to the delight of audiences packed into large venues throughout the nation.

It became common for male employees meeting at the water cooler or in the coffee room on Monday mornings to describe their weekend antics as what could be expected from a "wild and crazy guy".

Now let's talk about Tucker Carlson.

A wild and crazy guy?

The button-down archconservative a wild and crazy guy?
You bet.

Here are just a few tales from the annals of Tucker Carlson, the wild and crazy guy.

It all begins with the freedom and free-for-all environment in the *Spin Room*. *The Spin Room* was Carlson's first TV gig with a regular repeating schedule. Carlson was the resident representative conservative put up against Bill Press, a long-suffering lefty serving as Carlson's counterpoint.

The two of them covered all the various topics of the day and they usually included appearances from guests to set the table for the discussion and act as a catalyst for debate.

Funny thing about this show was that it was somewhat early in the evolution of cable television political talk programs and for this reason was quite lacking in structure.

That CNN was not spending a lot of money on the production not only meant that the show was taped on a cheap set but it also meant that the cable network did not spend a lot of time or money tracking down appropriate guests.

As result, Carlson and Press sometimes didn't know who the guest was going to be until the last minute because production assistants were unable to find people willing to appear on the program. They did occasionally get some big names but just as often the guest was an unknown, frequently unsophisticated and without much knowledge of the topic at hand.

Carlson and Press forged ahead however and despite their political differences became good friends in this unstructured and somewhat freewheeling environment.

Press and Carlson became friends partly because both

men enjoyed the idea that they could move the program in whatever direction suited them.

If you really want some amusement, look for the archives where Dr. Ruth Westheimer makes multiple appearances discussing sexual practices. Bill Press seems to roll with the punches while Tucker seems a little bit uncomfortable releasing his now well-known high-pitched laugh.

In one segment, Dr. Ruth asked Tucker to promise her that he will engage in the sex practice suggested during the show and report back to her the reaction to the practice from Tucker's bride.

In another segment Dr. Ruth turned to the two male hosts and told them that she was able to envision the two of them with their respective wives engaging in a Dr. Ruth recommended sexual practice. You can see Carlson blushing on camera. *The Spin Room* was a different kind of show.

Because *The Spin Room* was a preciously unsupervised production, Bill Press and Tucker Carlson realized that there were many viewers across the country subject to the slightest subtle suggestion when it came to sending gifts to the hosts.

Tucker Carlson and Bill Press learned how to gently create a discussion of various products. The mention of the product was always generic to prevent them from providing free advertising to some manufacturer. Nonetheless, a mere mention usually resulted in postal packages delivered to Press and Carlson containing all manner of tchotchkes or even small appliances.

The situation might develop something like this. Making small talk at the beginning or end of the show, Press would tell Carlson that he was having a hard time finding a baseball cap that fit him properly. Carlson would sympathize with the problem and maybe agree that it was hard to find a good baseball cap.

Within a week or two, devotees of the show would send caps of all colors displaying logos from high school, college, or major league teams.

As time went on, the situation almost got out of control. Bill press doing *The Spin Room* was a little bit like shopping. If the hosts were willing to be patient, they could mention a needed item during their small talk and sooner or later the wish would be fulfilled, and another item checked off the shopping list.

You would've thought that the network would've caught on to this little game, but the supervisory production staff was too busy doing other things to notice this little scheme.

Carlson thought this whole thing with the viewer gifts was pretty wild but unlike his partner in crime, Tucker drew the line at food.

Tucker's philosophy was that these little food freebies could do harm, especially since there could be potential digestive pain. Carlson believed that it was a bad idea to partake of the food items frequently delivered to the set from viewers reacting to the ramblings of the two hosts.

Bill Press, on the other hand, loved the home-cooked brownies, cakes, cookies, pies, and other consumables arriving from across the country. While Carlson wasn't taking any chances, Bill Press could wolf down a strawberry *Cassata* cake like a German Shepherd. Carlson kept a close eye on Bill Press when this happened to see if his cohost was looking green in the gills. He was always fine. He must've had an iron stomach.

Cohost Bill Press was a master at this game and even

found a way to maneuver his way to a few free meals. The guy was a genius, and this is how he did it.

Press would respond to a friendly question from Carlson by talking about one of his favorite vacation spots. But then Bill Press would elaborate naming specific restaurants and talking about the delicious nature of trademark menu items that made the whole trip so enjoyable.

Bill press was providing free restaurant advertising on national television. The next time he traveled to that vacation spot, the restaurant owners rewarded

Bill Press was a worthy liberal foil for Tucker. They became fast friends. Carlson crowned him the King of getting free stuff.

him for his kind words. Some even suspected that Bill Press could go on a long vacation and never spend a penny on food. Bill press was lovable… and smart.

Another feature of the disorganized nature of the loosely produced *Spin Room* involved the great ceramic mug debate. Back in the days of *The Spin Room* and true in relation to the talk shows of the present day, it was not uncommon for the hosts to sip coffee from a ceramic mug emblazoned with the talk show logo.

Press and Carlson continuously dropped hints to the sparsely populated production crew but to no avail. Carlson and Press were beginning to feel that their program was not respected by the network. They were right, and the requests for the highly prized ceramic mugs continued to fall on deaf ears.

Eventually, the pressure surrounding the great ceramic mug controversy was too much. Carlson called the public relations department for CNN who informed him that *The Spin Room* budget did not leave room for ceramic mugs. Carlson was shocked and somewhat offended that the network viewed the program as so unimportant that it didn't even qualify for two-dollar ceramic mugs.

The PR director told Tucker to contact the CNN gift shop director in Atlanta to see if anything else could be done. Tucker dutifully called the number given to him by the public relations professional. The number had been disconnected and it was then that Carlson realized that CNN management viewed *The Spin Room* as a big nothing.

It was quite a shock to his ego but when he told Bill Press about the situation, Bill shrugged and then slyly suggested that they talk about specific expensive restaurants as part of their opening chatter.

Another interesting thing about Tucker Carlson is that when he finds something interesting he wants to do more than just talk about it. He wants to actually do the activity that is the subject of the discussion. He likes to take things that are of theoretical interest and bring them to life through personal experience.

Never has that been more true than with his peculiar intriguing attraction to the *potato cannon*.

At age 35 a curious Tucker Carlson came across an amazing device called a potato cannon. It consists of a long section of PVC pipe with the chamber at the bottom filled with some sort of aerosol propellant. When you ignite the propellant, the explosive pressure will shoot out of that pipe anything and everything that may be in the tube.

Idaho potatoes are one of the favorite projectiles and thus

the name. However, pretty much anything loaded in the tube will find itself airborne and traveling at a speed like some modern weapon. It is a truly dangerous toy as the potatoes have been known to easily penetrate drywall at the distance of 375 yards.

Tucker entertained his own children with hours of potato cannon demonstrations placing a vast array of objects into the tube for launching. Balls of all shapes, metal objects, and even rocks. Tucker was careful to supervise as he realized that the potato cannon could easily kill someone within firing range of the device.

But within Tucker Carlson there still remains a curious and mischievous little kid. He might've been 35 years old but his son's suggestion that they launch one of his daughter's Barbie dolls was just too enticing of an idea.

The Canon worked just as hoped with Barbie flying through the air like a superhero with the added little detail that her hair was on fire because of the igniting of the aerosol propellant. The entire neighborhood was impressed with the feat and even his daughters thought the event was so spectacular that the old Barbie doll was a worthy sacrifice.

By this time, neighborhood kids and passersby formed a little crowd excited about this almost military display of explosive might. This was one of the most exciting things that had happened in this neighborhood in a long time.

Carlson asked the girls to offer up one more Barbie doll so that the spectacular feat could be repeated. Tucker had everyone stand back as he installed the aerosol propellant and loaded Ken's girlfriend from *Mattel* into the chamber. He lit the igniter and waited for Barbie to take flight into neighborhood history.

When nothing happened, he told everyone to wait. With

the crowd keeping its distance, he opened the ignition chamber for full inspection.

And then he did something really stupid. He pulled the ignition trigger and all the explosive firepower of the aerosol propellant went in an unintended direction. Instead of sending Barbie for a ride, the exploding propellant shot out right at Tucker's face.

It was a dangerous maneuver and Tucker is lucky he wasn't killed. However, his eyebrows and his hair were significantly burned as were various other portions of his head. But his kids still cherish the comical memory of what their dad Tucker Carlson looked like at the scene of that accident.

It was reminiscent of that seen in *Home Alone* where Joe Pesci opens up a booby-trapped door only to discover that a burning blowtorch was setting his head on fire.

If you get a chance *Google* that movie and find the frames where Pesci has had his head set on fire and puts out the flames by sticking his head in the snow. That scene makes us laugh and I'm sure the memory of Tucker's potato cannon carelessness generates a few hilarious memories as well.

Thank God Tucker recovered and for television viewers thank God his lustrous head of hair grew back in place.

Tucker Carlson still loves potato cannons. Remember my theory that when Carlson finds something interesting, he requires that he himself personally participate in the interesting action.

In the case of the potato cannon, Carlson took the whole thing one step further and tracked down the potato cannon guru Joel Surprise in Appleton, Wisconsin. He interviewed him in what might be described as the potato cannon testing center of the universe. Joel Surprise is what Tucker Carlson describes as the Henry Ford of the potato cannon business. Tucker Carlson embedded himself in the potato cannon experimental testing center where the guru attempted any and all variations in terms of materials and in terms of reconfiguration of the potato cannon design.

He even created a powerful potato cannon bazooka which could be hoisted upon your shoulder and fired like a surface to air stinger missile. The *Spudtech* technology center doesn't look like much from the outside but on the inside there's an efficient factory where the very highest quality and most powerful potato cannons are manufactured for public consumption.

You see, for Tucker Carlson the examination of an object or subject remains incomplete unless he can penetrate every single dimension of the topic. If he were to become interested in a story about horses, he would soon be feeding them, riding them, raising them, and maybe even sleeping in the barn with them. Tucker is a great writer because he refuses to limit his work to merely scratching the surface.

That's one of the reasons why in some ways he is feared as a media personality. Everyone knows that Tucker will penetrate to the core of every person, place, or thing he is covering. If you are a public figure and you consent to an interview, be prepared because Tucker will know all your secrets before the interview begins.

It's just the way he is about everything. He doesn't just write a story: he becomes obsessed with it until the article is filed or the broadcast is finally made on air. And then on to the next project.

And now a word about Tucker Carlson and drinking. As you read previously, sometimes following a political campaign is like doing a bar hop going from one tavern to another as the evening progresses.

Tucker Carlson is not a heavy drinker but when the campaign drinks the reporters drink. The previous discussion in this book about the McCain campaign shows the way that there can be a close relationship between the success of the campaign and availability of a well-stocked bar. The McCain presidential tour bus and plane were legendary for their free-flowing booze and talented bartenders. The drinks were always free, and it really did make for a party atmosphere during that campaign.

Back in the days when Tucker Carlson was chasing different stories all across the United States, he frequently found himself in airport taverns waiting for the next flight frequently delayed or stuck in a long layover.

Alcohol usually made it easier to sleep on the flight and Tucker was like all the other reporters who realized that anything that made travel a little bit easier was a good idea in the highly competitive world of news journalism.

Carlson never succumbed to the dangers of alcoholism, but he did see many of his friends in the world of chasing news stories fall prey to the dangers of over indulgence. In other words, Tucker Carlson knew how to drink, when to drink, and when to stop.

It takes a certain degree of discipline, but he realized a long time ago that quality writing is usually a direct function of sobriety.

Only once did Carlson have the misfortune of drinking a little too much intersect with his communications with the public. Back in 1996, Carlson attended an after-election party in a very famous hotel suite. The election was not very exciting as Bob Dole was getting crushed by the Bill Clinton machine on its way to a second term.

Tucker Carlson had finished all his work for the night and the rowdy crowd of mostly Republicans enjoyed the evening with good friends and good booze. The Republicans had read the polls and knew that they were going to get demolished, so the theme of the evening was one of enjoyment and anticipation of the next electoral project.

In other words, everybody knew Dole was going to lose, so it was important to have a good time. Carlson was just one of a handful of reporters attending the festivities.

The people at the party were great and the alcohol was of the very highest quality. These people knew how to throw a shindig. Tucker got lost in his thoughts and was even feeling a little bit tipsy. He made arrangements for a driver so he knew he would make it safely to his bed that night.

Suddenly, he remembered that he was scheduled to do a remote radio interview on National Public Radio that very same evening. Carlson found an unoccupied bedroom in the hotel suite and called into the radio station to give his expert opinion on the events of the day.

Soon radio listeners heard a very strange exchange. The radio host tried to get Tucker Carlson to focus on the significance of the Clinton victory.

The soused Tucker Carlson would have none of it and instead wanted to discuss the historical significance of all the weird things that had taken place in that hotel suite years prior when Clinton advisor Dick Morris spent time with a call girl in that very same suite.

The stunned radio interviewer tried but failed to elicit some grain of political insight from the renowned Tucker

Carlson. The radio personality went to a break and Tucker hung up.

Carlson is not known as a heavy drinker, and he is not. But that night was not a good time for the interview. See, Tucker Carlson is not that much different from you and me. He's a highly talented newsman dedicated to his family. But occasionally, just like the rest of us, he has a bad night.

Sometime in the early 2000s, Carlson gave up drinking altogether. He really didn't have to but like so many of the projects undertaken by Carlson, he engages in a detailed risk versus reward analysis.

Liquor could be enjoyable on occasion but it wasn't that great and certainly not worth another NPR interview from the Dick Morris suite that could hurt his career. This happy journalist warrior has a practical side that keeps him out of trouble.

This last story about Tucker in this chapter has to do with the time that his substantial writing skills were pressed into service in an unadvisable way.

It's a neat story but it goes back to Carlson's senior year at Trinity College in Hartford, Connecticut.

It seems that one of Tucker's roommates was about to fail an important Economics class for failure to attend class. The roommate was an extremely intelligent fellow quite capable of thoroughly studying the text and then passing the final exam without having attended a single lecture.

That's when the trouble started. The Econ professor in question told the young man that his non-attendance would keep him from passing even if he scored a perfect 100% on the written exam. Tucker's roommate was in a panic as he realized that missing those classes would keep him from graduating, even if he understood the subject matter better than the professor did.

Tucker Carlson, though only a college senior, had already developed pretty good writing chops, even penning a few articles for the school newspaper.

Tucker's desperate friend developed a plan, but he needed someone to skillfully compose a letter. The two of them created a very real-looking letterhead from the desk of a psychologist whose existence was a product of the two boys' imagination.

The letter, which was directed to the Economics professor, outlined a detailed diagnosis of the psychological problems encountered by Tucker's roommate Bill. The letter gave a brief history which today would be considered a violation of medical confidentiality laws. The letter was very professional and very convincing.

The letter also presented the potential for a positive outcome if certain requirements could be satisfied. Essentially, wrote Dr. X, Bill would be able to conquer his demons if only those superior to him could give him the opportunity to succeed.

The letter was a subtle request that the professor allow Bill to sit for the test and graduate if the test score demonstrated that Bill grasped the subject matter. Tucker knew that the brilliant Bill was so smart that he could probably teach the class himself.

The two miscreants sent the fake letter to the Dean who immediately realized the seriousness of the situation. The letter was so good in describing the condition that the Dean was alarmed that such a disturbed young man was living on campus.

The fabulous letter forced the University to throw Bill out

because they were afraid to have such a severe mental case roaming the hallowed halls of the University.

Eventually Bill found his way to graduate and established a great career for himself.

What the story really proves is that Tucker Carlson is a great writer and sometimes so good that he is too good.

Like I said at the beginning of this chapter, you can love Tucker Carlson because he really is a wild and crazy guy.

And he is just like the rest of us and that's why we love him.

CHAPTER 28
SWEET MYSTERIES OF LIFE

I n 1937 film stars Nelson Eddy and Jeanette McDonald recorded a song that was a big hit from one of their movie musicals, a song called *Sweet Mysteries Of Life*.

This chapter in relation to Tucker Carlson could also be about one of the mysteries of life because it details Tucker Carlson's admiration for one of the most famous Democrat party consultants in history by the name of James Carville.

Carville is a fascinating character. With his clean-shaven head and almost albino skin tone, his eyes are deep set hidden by a furrowed brow accented by high angular cheekbones and a mouth that seems always ready to threaten the exposure of fangs.

Tucker Carlson has described Carville's appearance as reptilian. This writer believes that Carville's facial features actually call to mind some kind of evil alien life form. Carville's features are so foreboding that when you watch him on television you half expect his eyeballs to glow red pulsing in an effort at the mind control necessary for his species to take over the planet Earth.

Carville hails from the deep South Cajun country and does little to hide the drawling accent that seems more appropriate for the overseer of a chain gang in the 1930s than from a popular political pundit. When you combine that strange appearance and the peculiar accent it is sort of frightening and yet fascinating at the same time.

Fascinating because this hard edged southern good ol' boy speaks on behalf of liberal policies that have been the driving force for the Democrat party for the last 40 years.

Carville's family had established deep roots in the South, running a popular general store in the town named after his grandfather in Carville, Louisiana. Unable to successfully endure the rigors of academia, Carville flunked out of Louisiana State University and served in the Marines for two years at Camp Pendleton in San Diego.

His brief military tour matured him significantly, and he buckled down and finally obtained his Bachelor of Science degree at LSU and even went on to get a law degree in 1973.

He worked for a Baton Rouge law firm for about six years until he realized that the field of politics really got his juices flowing.

He then began to bounce around serving in different roles on behalf of various campaigns over the next several years. He had some victories, and he had a whole lot of losses but the important thing was that Carville was learning the business of politics and campaigns, and not always working on behalf of Democrats.

This was an important part of his political education as you learn that political victories frequently were more a function of political technique than of ideology.

At age 40 in 1984, Carville's success as a political strategist was highly unimpressive and Carville was filled with self-doubt when it came to his future.

However, beginning with the Pennsylvania gubernatorial race in 1986, Carville rang up a string of impressive political victories, running the race for governor in Pennsylvania, Kentucky, Georgia, and Texas. In the course of six years of various statewide races he had emerged from the ashes of defeat into one of the most sought-after political directors in the country.

Carville was ready to move on to a national race and the opportunity came along when Bill Clinton asked Carville to take the reins of his presidential bid in 1992. Defeating an incumbent president is never easy but Carville's masterful direction of the Clinton campaign in its defeat of the elder George Bush is still a master study in political science. Bush had the advantage of operating in the reflected glow of the wildly popular former President Ronald Reagan.

However, Carville found a crack in the Bush armor developing the now famous "it's the economy stupid" slogan for the campaign. Carville's strategy depicted the elder Bush as living in an ivory tower detached from the economic woes of the average American.

Clinton was the perfect foil against the highbrow Kennebunkport elitist image of his opponent. In fact, Carville liked it when people began calling Clinton "Bubba" because the nickname told citizens that Clinton was like them, far from the aristocratic Republicans who never saw the inside of a Walmart.

Clinton's victory now meant that Carville had arrived, and his stock rose even further with Clinton's convincing reelection victory in the face of the Monica Lewinsky scandal that Republicans fully relied on in hopes of defeating Clinton.

The surprising Clinton reelection secured Carville's place in campaign history. Carville capitalized on the success by joining the lecture circuit commanding lecture fees that soon made him a millionaire. He then began cranking out books which became bestsellers authored by the ultimate political Guru.

It is during this phase of Carville's career that he and Tucker Carlson began to cross paths. Carville was now beginning to establish a persona as the ultimate Democrat party media pundit just as Carlson's career was taking off in the same way from a Republican perspective.

As result, Carlson found himself on camera debating hundreds of issues with the "Ragin' Cajun" as Carville was beginning to become known.

The two men were together so often in so many different forums that they formed a friendship. They were friendly foes who disagreed with one another while admiring the skills of their opponent.

The fascinating thing about all this is that Carlson has written about Carville and expounded on his abilities and political positions. However, Carlson curiously describes Carville as an actor playing a role in order to make money.

Tucker Carlson believes that Carville is deep down a conservative Catholic who is playacting as an overly dramatic left-wing Democrat activist.

This playacting sells books and earns him appearances on television that not only increases book sales but gives him the opportunity for gigs on the lecture circuit.

In other words, Carville is an effective left-wing pundit well-paid to project himself as a left-wing pundit.

But because Carlson knows the real Carville, he is friends with Carville and in fact admires the real Carville because he doesn't try to engage in playacting when dealing with Carlson one on one.

Scary-looking and brilliant, Carville is one of Tucker's closest confidants.

Carlson is friends with Carville because Carville lets down his guard in his private relationship with Carlson, his friend.

Carlson himself is an important national figure and that means it is difficult to know who your real friends are and know who you can trust. Carlson knows that his friend James Carville must project this rough-edged maniac left-wing persona in order to make a living.

Carlson is happy to accept that truth because the real James Carville behind the mask is a true-blue friend with whom Carlson has much in common in terms of basic values and the way that one lives one's life.

Tucker Carlson's justifiable friendship with Carville is completely believable when you look at Carville's marriage.

Carville is married to one of our countries high-powered Republican strategists, Mary Matalin. Unsophisticated observers would find such a marriage unimaginable because it would seem impossible for the hard charging sometimes crude Democrat strategist to be united with the right wing Mary Matalin.

Carville himself once told a reporter from *U.S. News and World Report* that the spectacular success of this marriage between polar political opposites was "unexplainable".

This of course brings us back to the discussion of the song *Sweet Mysteries Of Life* that opened up this chapter.

Tucker Carlson appears to be one of those people who, like Mary Matalin, can bore down to the authentic core of not just issues, but of people.

Carlson loves and trusts the inner core of James Carville despite the nutty aggressive exterior.

It is one of the sweet mysteries of life.

CHAPTER 29
RACE

Tucker Carlson has been called a white supremacist. In fact, *New York Times* reporter Nicholas Confessore wrote a series of articles about Tucker Carlson and analyzed upwards of 1100 broadcasts of *Tucker Carlson Tonight*. Nicholas assembled a number of his associate reporters at the *Times* in order to prepare a microscopic analysis of the Carlson television content.

Nicholas told National Public Radio that Carlson "has constructed what may be the most racist show in the history of cable news".

How did a television personality with legitimate journalistic credentials and who openly professes his Christian faith get hit with the racist label?

First of all, it begins with the fact that Tucker Carlson's view of race is frozen in time. Tucker Carlson repeatedly harkens back to Martin Luther King in his famous "I Have a Dream" speech in which King declares that the ideal for our country is that people should be judged by the content of their character and not by the color of their skin.

The speech was delivered by MLK in 1963 at the foot of the Lincoln Memorial. Tucker Carlson wasn't born until 1969 but throughout his career as a writer and political commentator he has made Dr. King's speech the touchstone of his racial philosophy.

Fast forward to 2023 and many in America consider the Martin Luther King philosophy to be dated and anachronistic. Those who believe that we must be blind to race and make it a nonfactor in sizing up our fellow Americans are deemed to be racist in an effort to be racially neutral.

Dr. martin Luther King, Tucker's North star on the subject of race.

Ibram X. Kendi, easily the most celebrated black author in the world on the subject of race, believes that race is an important ingredient in pursuit of racial justice.

In other words, writes X. Kendi, white people must be judged as racists because they are white and black people must be judged as victims because they are black. X. Kendi argues that we live in a world of built-in injustice where white people are all prejudiced by virtue of their skin and where black people are their victims.

In addition to Ibram X. Kendi, the other major denialist of Dr. King is a black author by the name of Ta-Nehisi Coates.

Ta-Nehisi Coates is without question a critic of Dr. Martin Luther King because Coates believes that equality is a racist concept. Therefore, argues Coates, the people who adhere to a compassionate concept of racial equality are actually racist themselves.

The arguments submitted by X. Kendi and by Coates have caught on throughout America in a way that makes MLK seem like a dinosaur. X. Kendi and Coates therefore attack adherence to racial equality as a racist objective founded on white supremacy.

Of course, these arguments defy logic and mock the sincere religious aspirations of Dr. King to change the hearts of men to the point where race becomes an irrelevant factor.

This new generation of civil rights activists pursue a view that justifies disdain of white people because of their skin color and argues for financial and other rewards be given to black people because of the color of their skin.

The loving race-neutral God of Martin Luther King has been replaced by a race-baiting God of judgment based on the color of your skin. Martin Luther King must be spinning in his grave.

Ta-Nehisi Coates despises Dr. King's dream of a equality because he believes that the dream "is an illusion of a quality that white Americans uphold in order to feel good about themselves and their country."

Believing in equality means ignoring inequality, so white America's peace of mind, says Coates, "comes at the expense of black America."

Under this new regime, Tucker Carlson begins with a disadvantage as he strives for equality and without regard to race. According to the new civil rights activists, Carlson is already pursuing a racist view.

The second area that has created racial criticism of Carlson is his blaming black out-of-wedlock birth rates for economic disparities between the races.

Black commentators call Carlson a white supremacist because he urged black Americans to adopt a culture of matrimony before reproduction.

This is completely unfair as the raw data supports Carlson here. In the 1950's, 17% of black births were the result of an unmarried union. The rate today is 73%, a stunning increase. Most importantly, there is a parallel between poverty and unwed births.

President Obama told black men to stop producing children without a marriage certificate as a way to create a culture of success for American black families. Don Lemon, one of Tucker's harshest critics, lectured his black viewers in 2013 with the following soliloquy:

> Just because you can have a baby, it doesn't mean you should, especially without planning for one or getting married first. More than 72 percent of children in the African-American community are born out of wedlock... that means absent fathers. And the studies show that lack of a male role model is an express train right to prison and the cycle continues.

And yet Carlson is called a racist when he repeats the views of Obama and CNN's Lemon.

The third item that has caused left-wing commentators to view Carlson as a racist is Carlson's exposing *replacement theory* as a political strategy.

Carlson has through the years described a strategy fomented by the Democrat party to win elections through the process of importing Democrats into the USA so that Republicans are easily outnumbered.

The New York Times analysis of Carlson's programs

referred to many examples were Carlson criticizes the strategy that Carlson proclaims to be a real detestable political plan.

The New York Times experts describe Carlson's theory as a racist conspiracy designed to create fear in the hearts of white voters.

The Times reporters say that Carlson continues to beat the drum over this replacement theory. *The Times* says this demonstrates that Carlson lies about anything to energize white supremacists in America.

The New York Times forgot just one thing. The replacement theory was not developed by Republicans but rather has been proclaimed as an actual game plan *by Democrats*.

In 2013, the left leaning Center For American Progress published a long form analysis outlining the way Democrats have intentionally used immigration to pump up voter rolls. The article is titled "Immigration is changing the political landscape in key States".

It provides the raw data of immigrants moving into red states and turning them blue almost overnight. California is a great example as the state that loved Ronald Reagan just a few years ago is now powerfully Democrat because of immigrant inflow. Even once solidly Republican New Hampshire is now Democrat territory because of immigration.

In 2018, former Obama HUD Secretary Julian Castro predicted that new immigrants will soon overtake Republicans to make the Lone Star State of Texas a Democrat stronghold.

Enter Democrat Senator Durbin. In July of 2019, Senator Dick Durbin said the following on the floor of the Senate:

The demographics of America are not on the side of the Republican Party. The new voters in this country are moving away from them, away from Donald Trump, away from their party creed that they preach.

In that same year Speaker of the House Nancy Pelosi celebrated the influx of immigrants because of the way *"demographics will weigh in politically."*

Politico, a favorite liberal media site, published an article describing the way immigrants would "transform the nation's political landscape for a generation or more…. with as many as 11 million new Hispanic voters coming into the electorate a decade from now in ways that current trends hold **producing an electoral bonanza for Democrats and crippling Republican prospects."**

Clearly Carlson's attempt to discuss the way that unregulated immigration easily transforms voting blocs is merely an honest discussion about what Democrats believe happens when millions of people across our borders.

Durbin and Pelosi are banking on electoral victories fueled by this quickly advancing increase in the immigrant population. As leftists, they are free to discuss this without repercussion.

But Tucker Carlson, as a conservative commentator, is unable to discuss the very same issue without being labeled a racist. Liberal democrats label Carlson and any other replacement theory proponents as racists while they embrace their own version of the policy.

It is hypocrisy being used to destroy your political enemies. *The New York Times* a long time ago gave up on the idea of honest reporting. The *Times* today is one of many communication instruments serving the will of the Democrat party.

That's one of the many reasons that Tucker Carlson is such an important part of the media landscape.

He absorbs unfair attacks of racism from the left and does not apologize. He stands his ground knowing that the truth will be his shield and the facts will be his sword.

Now that's what I call a warrior.

CHAPTER 30
I LIKE IKE

Tucker Carlson has on numerous occasions said that the ideal for the American citizen is nothing really very ambitious. The average American and Tucker Carlson merely seek to have the chance to live a reasonable life through a job that makes it possible without interference from the government or anyone else.

This ideal life also includes a society in which everyone, including the media and government, tell the truth and where government listens to the needs of the people and tries to satisfy those needs.

To some extent, Carlson is pointing to the American life as lived by our citizens in the 1950s.

This was the Eisenhower era. This part of American history had flaws to be sure but it seemed that the American values of honesty, hard work, and respect for the opinion of others were blossoming like never before in American history.

To this writer, the President Eisenhower years seemed

closer to the idyllic life that Carlson has described than the present day.

Carlson is troubled that the ruling elite continuously ignore the needs of the average citizen and they do this on a bipartisan basis. Carlson knows that Americans merely want to adequately support their families and educate their children in a safe and wholesome environment.

Whether we want to admit it or not, America in the 1950s fulfilled its promise to its citizens much more effectively than it does today.

It is right to call attention to the racial unfairness of the 1950s, especially the deep South where Jim Crow was alive and well.

However, many overlook the fact that America in the 1950s gave birth to many of the civil rights that came to full flower in the 1960s under the leadership of Dr. Martin Luther King.

Historians rightly point to the watershed event in the passage of the 1964 Civil Rights Act to bring America into the modern age of racial justice.

Unfortunately, most forget that the civil rights movement from a legislative standpoint really took wing under the leadership of President Eisenhower in 1957 with the passage of the 1957 Civil Rights Act. This landmark legislation created the civil rights division within the United States Justice Department and the created the opportunity for federal courts to protect minority voting rights. This law also established *The United States Civil Rights Commission* and gave it the power to investigate acts of discrimination.

The 1950s also gave us the United States Supreme Court which struck down the concept of separate but equal which for so many years had been used as an excuse for Jim Crow practices.

In the case of *Brown versus the Board of Education,* the 1954 Supreme Court told us that separate but equal was a fiction excusing discrimination and that same court ordered desegregation of our school systems.

Present Eisenhower himself intervened on behalf of minority students when he sent federal troops to Little Rock, Arkansas to protect black children attempting to attend classes with their white brothers and sisters.

So dedicated to changing the hearts and minds of American citizens was President Eisenhower that he received the full throated endorsement of Democrat Congressman Adam Clayton Powell Junior, the first black congressman from New York and the proud representative of Harlem.

Congressman Powell wrote the following:

This (passage of the 1957 Civil Rights Act) vindicates my support of President Eisenhower regardless of what may happen to me. Personally, I am proud to have campaigned for one who has kept every word to me. After 80 years of political slavery, this is the second emancipation.

A dynamic outspoken black congressman endorsing a Republican president was quite an unusual event. This again however illuminates the fact that the 1950s really were a time for hope and change but hope and change that was taking place in the context of a decent society.

That's really what Tucker Carlson is looking for. A decent society. In today's world the formerly respected *New York Times* is the most dishonest print media in America and if you disagree with their woke agenda, keep your mouth shut or they will seek to have you lose your job.

Can we ever reach the level of decency of the 1950s and do it in a way that protects minority rights along with treating people with loving kindness and forgiveness?

Tucker Carlson believes in American exceptionalism and is guardedly optimistic in his belief that American greatness comes from a source spiritual or perhaps even divine.

Otto von Bismarck said that "God has a special providence for fools, drunkards, and the United States of America."

Given the disintegration of the American family and our patriotic values, this ideal seems more out of reach perhaps more so than at any time in our history.

Adam Clayton Powell was a dynamic congressman, the first black representative from Harlem. An outspoken Democrat and civil rights activist, he loved Eisenhower and the decency Powell saw from Republicans in the 1950's.

We may never get there but Tucker Carlson is doing his best to publish the truth and to force government officials to listen to the people.

Eisenhower himself, of course, being human, had plenty of flaws. But he was a decent man who reflected an era of decency.

We likely will never see another Eisenhower but with Tucker Carlson behind a microphone we still have a shot at a decent caring civilized community.

CHAPTER 31
F BOMBS AWAY

Tucker Carlson's credentials as an independent thinker make you realize that he is his own man. His success grows out of his willingness to attack Republican gospel with the same vigor with which he goes after the Democrats.

Never was this more obvious than when he separated himself from Republican bigwigs in an article that he wrote for *Talk Magazine* in 1999.

Let me set the scene for you. George W. Bush was in the middle of a huge fundraising swing throughout the country in 1999 as he set himself up as the odds-on favorite to become the Republican nominee for president in the year 2000.

As governor of Texas, Bush had carved out for himself a perception that he was a different kind of Bush from his father George Bush the elder who served as Reagan's VP and then was elected to a single term as president, only to lose to young and dynamic William Jefferson Clinton in 1992.

Bush accomplished this feat by painting himself as a real Texan in contrast to the highbrow Kennebunkport, Maine personality of his father.

Bush the elder presented himself as a coolheaded intellectual government insider who governed well because of his years of experience leading various government agencies including the CIA.

Bush the younger wanted to be photographed at his ranch wearing denim outfits and cowboy boots, breaking a sweat digging post holes for fences and herding livestock.

While George W. was more of an outdoorsman than his father, this man of the earth caricature was basically a lie. George the younger was definitely his father's son, having attended Ivy League universities and having made his wealth in the oil industry that also made his father rich. The younger Bush served in the Texas Air National Guard as a way of avoiding regular military service which might have gotten in the way of his young man desires to chase women and get drunk on weekends.

But what the younger Bush really had going for him was an authentic Texas swagger. He oozed confidence so much so that his sometimes-inarticulate way of speaking was endearingly interpreted as coming from a man so firm in his convictions that he was in no hurry to spit out his words.

It was reminiscent of the acting style of Gary Cooper in the 1940s and 1950s. Cooper used to deliver his lines with slow deliberation that at first made it seem like he was a slow thinker. But after listening to him for a while you realized that the slow delivery of the words really conveyed confidence in the truth of those words. It was intoxicating to the listener.

This was part of the mystique of George W. Bush. He also had a way of moving his shoulders as he made his way into a room that created a John Wayne sense of machismo. Once when a reporter asked him about this Bush responded with a smile, "this is what we refer to in Texas as 'walking' ".

So as the year 1999 was coming to an end, Tucker Carlson was given permission to embed himself in the George Bush campaign. The Bush people were happy to accommodate Carlson as the new political reporter for a new publication called *Talk Magazine*.

They knew Carlson to be a snappy writer, but they also knew that he was a conservative thinker who had aligned himself with Bush the elder in prior years.

The Bush family was familiar with Carlson because of their interactions with him when Carlson was nothing but a puppy reporter during the Reagan-Bush era. The George W. Bush campaign was confident that they had nothing to worry about with the button-down Tucker Carlson hanging around.

They were wrong about that.

George W. wasn't afraid to let down his guard throughout that two-week period as Carlson shadowed him from one campaign or fundraising event to another. The future president was certain that little bits of negative information encountered by Carlson on the campaign trail would never find their way into print when Carlson finally turned his notes into a polished story.

They were exceptionally wrong about that as well.

Here's what happened.

Tucker Carlson was given 100% access to George W. Bush during a frenetic couple of weeks where "W" was trying to nail down votes for the upcoming presidential primary simultaneous to attending large donor fundraisers.

Carlson had numerous opportunities to interview campaign staffers and more importantly had several one-on-one conversations with Bush between functions on tour buses, limousines, and up in the air on Bush's campaign jet.

The resulting article contained three pieces of information that damaged the Bush campaign effort.

The first one was Carlson's description of Bush's liberal use of the word "Fuck" in conversation. Remember that this article was published in 1999 when it would be unusual for a candidate profile to include repeating the candidate's use of the term in print. These days F bombs have become *de rigueur* on cable television and even in many mainstream publications.

But back then this created quite a stir. Bush fashioned himself a serious Christian and Carlson's repeating the word as coming from the lips of the future president turned out to be shocking for many of Bush's evangelical followers.

In the end, Tucker's F bomb revelation did not keep Bush out of the White House but at the time many thought it was a serious misstep to give Carlson access to the real George W. Bush vocabulary.

In some circles, this article became known as "The F bomb article" and was held up as an example of Bush being crude and careless.

The F bomb article contained a second piece of information that was also alarming to Bush's handlers.

The State of Texas had executed Carla Fay Tucker after she was convicted of committing a double murder. As she waited on death row, celebrities and anti-death penalty groups launched a series of protests designed to pressure Bush into granting clemency to stop the execution.

Bianca Jagger, wife of *Rolling Stones* founder Mick Jagger, led a number of these protests and stormed the State Capitol in Austin, Texas to force Bush to stop the execution.

At that time, talk show host Larry King was at the height of his powers and he interviewed the murderess on national television where she made a plaintive plea asking Bush to spare her life.

Bush assumed Carlson would write a puff piece. He was wrong.

Bush arrogantly and almost proudly told Carlson that he refused to meet with any of the protesters, determined to see the State of Texas carry out its duty to rid the world of dangerous criminals.

During the Larry King interview, King asked Carla Fay Tucker if she had anything to say to the Texas governor. She looked into the camera and asked for mercy. Carlson, not having seen the interview, asked George W. Bush about what the death row inmate had said to King.

Tucker Carlson wrote that Bush assumed a mocking tone and an artificial voice in telling Carlson that the woman whimpered "please don't kill me".

This part of the article painted Bush as callous and unthoughtful in the face of the young woman begging for her life. Many media pundits wondered if such a hardened unthinking man should be allowed anywhere near the nuclear codes that could possibly lead to the end of civilization.

Again, this little dialogue did not stand in the way of Bush taking residence at 1600 Pennsylvania Avenue, but it did cause some voters to pause contemplating what kind of man had such a crass attitude toward human life.

In some sectors of the Republican Party, though, this over-the-top tough guy approach actually earned supporters for

Bush as thousands of pro-death penalty voters decided they had found their man.

Bush tried to downplay this remark in the general election campaign but that wasn't so easy to do. Carlson's story was described during the campaign against Al Gore as a demonstration that Bush lacked compassion and the ability to think things through with calm deliberation. Gore told the world that Bush was a knee-jerk overreactor and that ultimately Bush lacked the ability to act with deliberation as president.

The third revelation coming from the pen of Carlson was a great contrast to the first two and to some extent it softened the blow of the first two even though at the time the Bush campaign operatives were very concerned.

Here's the way it happened. Bush was on the campaign bus reading a handwritten letter sent to him by former President Bush the elder. Apparently the letter, described by Carlson as "particularly touching", affected the reader deeply as it was filled with emotion, father to son.

Carlson encountered George Bush finishing off the letter and then weeping openly. It was simply a moment when the pressures and tensions of a national campaign found a release for the candidate as he read his father's tender words.

That release came in the form of a crying jag that I suspect would've resulted in any one of us who read such a letter from a loving parent amid the bitter dogfight of a national campaign.

Bush was furious. He trusted Carlson but now Carlson was writing about a moment that was much too personal to be included in a nationally published profile. Many of the Bush aides complained that the tough guy image they had worked so hard to build was disintegrating in the face of this remarkable scene on the campaign bus.

Again, this third amazing feature of the F bomb article obviously did not keep victory away from Bush. There were a few in the campaign inner circle who saw the crying incident as a way of smoothing over some of the rough edges of Bush's tough guy act.

Cynics proclaimed that the tears were not genuine, and that Bush was acting, an Academy Award-winning performance designed to tell voters that the Texas governor really was a caring human being. These observers realized that Bill Clinton rode the phrase "I feel your pain" all the way to presidential victory. The crying act, they thought, was a good way to tap into the part of the electorate looking for an empathetic compassionate man.

In any case, Tucker Carlson demonstrated himself to be a truly tough and independent-minded member of the fourth estate.

Tucker Carlson proved that he would always be brutally honest in communicating with the public even if that meant alienating a man who was sure to become president. Tucker Carlson just didn't care, and this attitude would serve him well as the years progressed.

Tucker Carlson was not going to shill for anybody.

CHAPTER 32
PRISONER OF WAR

A s if the reader of this book didn't already understand that Tucker Carlson is a true man of adventure, this story will really drive home the point.

Tucker Carlson became a POW in Vietnam.

You read that right. Tucker was held prisoner in Vietnam, unable to escape.

There's quite a back story so let's get started.

Tucker Carlson had a history with Senator John McCain. In fact, it's fair to say that Carlson's experiences with McCain led him to admire the senator from the State of Arizona.

First of all, Tucker Carlson admired McCain because he was a real war hero. Shot down over Vietnam, McCain became the most famous prisoner of the infamous Hanoi Hilton.

McCain was seriously injured when he hit the eject button from his P-55 aircraft which was going down in flames having taken on surface to air gunfire.

In fact, McCain's injuries were so severe that the communist soldiers had to carry him to a crude medical facility where he was soon encased in some sort of primitive body cast.

McCain did not receive the nutrition needed for proper healing and the North Vietnamese even worsened the injury by setting McCain's bones at odd angles in order to encourage poor healing, leaving McCain with lifelong pain in his limbs.

Even after the removal of the cast, McCain was beaten mercilessly more so than other prisoners because McCain's father was a high-ranking admiral in the United States Navy.

McCain passed up the chance for early release from this prison camp because he insisted that prisoners be released in the order in which they were captured. It's a system of honor that says first-in-first-out, a form of noble accounting system related to human inventory in prison camps.

McCain really was heroic.

The beatings and the psychological torture took its toll on all the prisoners, but McCain endured, frequently mocking his captors at every opportunity. He knew that it would lead to more torture, but he felt morally obligated to antagonize the evil prison guards.

In one instance, when prisoners were rounded up so the Vietcong could create a propaganda film showing happy prisoners, McCain refused to cooperate. The photograph released to the American press by the North Vietnamese showed McCain giving the middle finger salute to the photographer.

In retribution, McCain was stabbed by his captors and had all his teeth knocked out. Despite this he persisted in his own form of psychological warfare by being a wise ass every chance he had. Years later he admitted that he had attempted suicide, knowing that his death would be difficult for the communists to explain.

McCain was heroic in so many ways during this period that it is difficult to imagine what he went through. Fast-forward to the presidential campaign in 2000. Tucker Carlson is embedded in the McCain campaign as he had been for so many campaigns in the past.

But Carlson discovers that the McCain campaign is unlike any other he has ever encountered. Instead of hanging out in an isolated area in the front of the bus on the front of the jet, McCain hangs out with the rest of the campaign workers and with all the media representatives throughout the totality of the campaign, only going into private meetings occasionally with his campaign staff.

The press eats this up. McCain is hanging out with reporters, reporters who have never ever had the chance to gain such familiarity with a presidential candidate. The result is that McCain was practically universally loved by the press corps that travels with him.

In addition to that, McCain does not put his guard up very often in communicating with his bus mates. McCain has a very salty vocabulary and uses it freely just like the wise ass personality who aggravated the North Vietnamese prison guards.

The reporters rarely repeat McCain's four-letter word remarks but they do praise his policy positions. They all look upon McCain as an earthy honest man whose war wounds earned him the right to run for the presidency of the country for which he shed his own blood.

The McCain entourage also includes a number of McCain's Vietnam War buddies, and this just adds to the devil-may-care *esprit de corps* that practically radiates from the McCain campaign group.

The McCain campaign also does one more thing that wins over the scribes. McCain makes certain that in the back of the bus and in the back the plane there is always a fully loaded professional style bar manned by a professional bartender. The drinks are always free and always high quality.

This was a brilliant strategy for John McCain. McCain was rising in the polls partially because newspaper and network reporters worshiped the man who was willing to say what was on his mind while providing the best of booze for media types constantly craving alcohol.

In addition, McCain made certain that his staff never made a fast-food run without providing plenty of free meals to the members of the fourth estate.

Covering the McCain campaign was a traveling party, and the partygoers loved the good times in the presence of their fearless leader. John McCain was Fonzie surrounded by Richie Cunningham, Potsy Weber, and Ralph Mouth who were groupies anxious to write great things about their idol, distributing positive candidate profiles to every media outlet in the world.

If the general election outcome could have been determined by the McCain press corps, Obama never would have been elected president.

Carlson marveled at McCain's two-pronged strategy when it came to the press. He wanted them to have complete and full access to the candidate and he wanted them to have all the creature comforts to keep them in a good mood.

It worked. Some of the press corps joked that McCain would've provided free call girls if he could've gotten away with it.

He didn't. But he certainly knew that having his campaign pick up the tab for booze and food would enhance his standing with the press.

On this trip, Carlson is again embedded with McCain. This time he was embedded with McCain's junket to Vietnam to visit some of the sites where atrocities were perpetrated against him almost 40 years prior.

The Vietnamese felt the awkwardness of the situation, but McCain was relaxed and talkative. He realized that evil men still controlled the Vietnamese peninsula, but he also realized that he could play a role in enhancing America's relationship with the Vietnam people if not the government of Vietnam.

McCain met with a number of officials and emphasized the desire to put the past behind him to build bridges with the American government.

McCain was not trying to undermine the Clinton administration, so he showed a certain degree of restraint.

He did, however, revert to form on occasion, snapping back at the officials with some kind of wise crack that the officials did not understand. Translations were not very good, and the Vietnamese did not quite understand what McCain was saying all the time.

On a couple of occasions, McCain could be seen smiling for the cameras, shaking hands with one of the officials while audibly calling the official a dumb ass. It was classic McCain. The officials assumed that the broad smile and a firm handshake meant that the Senator was paying them a compliment of some sort.

Carlson and other media representatives from America did not give away the joke until they got home. McCain the smart mouth war hero was now McCain smart mouth international ambassador. This was a man authentic from beginning to end.

And that's when Tucker Carlson's prisoner of war saga began to emerge. It was time for the McCain group to return home. A standard passport review by the Vietnamese officials revealed that Carlson's passport lacked the entry stamp that should've been placed on the passport when Carlson arrived in the country.

The Vietnamese official explained that no one could leave the country unless the entry stamp had been placed on the passport.

Carlson immediately knew what had happened. The Vietnamese had been working overtime to translate and interpret the remarks made by McCain at their various meetings.

Apparently, just before the American delegation was ready to leave, the Vietnamese realized what "dumb ass" meant and that McCain while mostly well behaved, had occasionally been making fools of his hosts.

Vietnam saw that there was nothing they could do about McCain himself as he was an important figure internationally.

But they could get a little bit of revenge by keeping one of the Americans from escaping back to the United States. Their victim was Tucker Carlson and as the Americans took off from the Saigon airport without him. Carlson had a sick feeling that he might be there for a long time.

McCain himself tried to intervene but since McCain was the one they were actually angry with, this had no impact.

Carlson learned at this time that the Vietnamese were also especially angry at McCain for a very brief statement he had issued at a press conference a couple of days earlier. McCain meant it as a throwaway line, but it was like a dagger to the hearts of the Vietnamese. McCain had told the gathered press as far as he was concerned "the wrong side had won the Vietnam War".

McCain, lower right, was an authentic war hero whose mouth was an effective weapon that got Tucker tossed into the slammer.

Now Carlson really understood what was going on. Straight talking wise acre John McCain had insulted his hosts, and now Carlson was a prisoner of war in this battle between American capitalism and despotic Chinese-sponsored communism. Carlson was now the only detainee in this modern prisoner of war camp.

After a few days, Carlson was rescued by President Clinton who dispatched a member of the State Department to negotiate Carlson's release.

It is unknown what leverage was employed to get Tucker out of Vietnam but one thing was clear. Tucker always found himself in tight spots and then turned the events into a great story. Carlson forgave McCain because he had great reverence for authentic war heroes.

Tucker admitted to himself that he wasn't exactly an inmate at the Hanoi Hilton like McCain many years prior. But still he often wonders what would've happened to him without the Hail Mary negotiation session from the Clinton State Department.

No matter.

Tucker Carlson still had many controversial stories to write about and still had his rise to fame at Fox News in his future.

CHAPTER 33
RAY EPPS

The case of Ray Epps is perhaps the very best example of something that makes Tucker Carlson truly a warrior when it comes to speaking truth to power.

Tucker Carlson does not back down in the face of opposition. In fact, he shows the kind of dogged determination in pursuit of a story that increases his energy in pursuit of that story as more hurdles are placed in his path.

It's kind of like a pit bull with a bone in his mouth. The more you try to pull that bone from the pit bull, the harder the pit bull will resist and clamp down on that bone as if life itself depended on keeping that bone in the clenches of his jaw.

Here's the story.

Within days of the alleged January 6 insurrection in 2021, hundreds of video clips appeared on *YouTube* and *Facebook* created by persons on the scene at the nation's capital during that dramatic event.

Some of the clips included a middle-aged man

encouraging protesters to enter into the Capitol building. Some of this video was filmed the night before January 6 and some of it was captured during various stages of the melee itself.

This middle-aged man, as can be seen in the video, is not shy about encouraging entry into the Capitol building. He is extremely specific and articulate in urging the Trump supporters to enter the building where Congress was conducting official proceedings to certify the presidential vote.

The video also captures this gentleman's tone. There was a real sense of urgency in his plea to the disenchanted Trump supporters.

He is seen pointing to the Capitol building and emphasizing the word "into" when directing them to go "into" the Capitol building.

It appears that he wants to make certain that no one misunderstands him by thinking that he only wants them to approach the building. He is emphatic that only entry into the hallowed halls of Congress will be satisfactory.

Ray Epps on January 6, 2021. NBC photo Kent Nishimura / Los Angeles Times via Getty Images file.

This is really suspicious in light of the fact January 6 prosecutors would later urge longer prison sentences for those that entered the building in comparison to those that remained outside.

It's almost as though this fellow understood the criteria for future criminal prosecutions and wanted to ensure the opportunity to jail Trump supporters in the days and weeks following this event.

The gentleman in question was a person by the name of Ray Epps.

Epps had been a regular member of an organization called the *Oathkeepers*. The FBI had infiltrated *Oathkeepers* for at least a couple of years prior to January 6 out of concern for militia groups opposing federal government authority.

Shortly after the events of January 6, the FBI published a list of persons of interest in their investigation of the January 6 "insurrection". It's a form of "most wanted" list of persons suspected of illegal activity against whom an arrest warrant had not yet been issued.

Not surprisingly, the name of Ray Epps was prominently featured on this list. After all, if the events of January 6 constituted an attempted violent overthrow of the American government, a person acting as a ringleader encouraging going into the Capitol would be a main target for criminal prosecution.

Several weeks later, as arrests of January 6 defendants began to pile up, Ray Epps remained at liberty and his name was removed from the notorious FBI persons of interest list.

This was curious.

Word began to circulate that the events of January 6 had

been fomented by undercover federal agents suggesting that protesters storm the capital building.

Ray Epps' name was prominently featured in these discussions since the video demonstrated his bombastic insistence that the protesters cross into the congressional building instead of waiting outside.

One section of the video even shows Trump supporters chanting "Fed... Fed... Fed!". Clearly people in the crowd viewed Ray Epps as some kind of FBI plant trying to get them into trouble by inciting criminal trespass.

These protesters were convinced that Ray Epps was engaging in entrapment, that is, inspiring a crime where none was otherwise contemplated.

As the Ray Epps undercover provocateur theory began to take shape, the government and the January 6 committee began to build a bunker around Ray Epps.

Mainstream media and Pelosi's handpicked January 6 committee interviewed Ray Epps in a nonpublic setting and emerged with a tale intended to exonerate him from any culpability whatsoever.

The New York Times even ran a story sympathetic to Ray Epps showing him to be an innocent party merely in the wrong place at the wrong time.

The January 6 committee then convened a formal deposition with Ray Epps placed under oath before the committee in another secret meeting of the committee.

The Times story and the deposition transcript show the reporters and handpicked Pelosi committee members straining to give Epps the chance to explain his activities as a convenient offramp to avoid criminal responsibility for what he did.

The problem is this. The bunker created by the media and

the January 6 committee merely emphasized questions concerning Epps's relationship with the FBI or other law enforcement authorities. The bunker was designed to eliminate the question of a conspiratorial relationship between Ray Epps and FBI agents.

Enter Tucker Carlson.

Carlson immediately recognized the national media Epps protection effort and the over-the-top gymnastics performed by the January 6 committee in an effort to insulate Epps.

Tucker Carlson would not be deterred and he decided to dig deeper into the truth. He examined the deposition given by Epps and the explanations he offered to the January 6 committee, said explanations swallowed whole by the January 6 committee and *The New York Times.*

Epps explained that his real intent was to diffuse the January 6 situation in order to diminish the chance for violence at the Capitol building. He explained that he was trying to gain the trust of the crowd so that he could then convince them to remain peaceful.

According to *The Times* and the members of January 6 committee, this eliminated the idea that Ray Epps served as a tool of the FBI. The Democrats seeking the scalp of Donald Trump proclaimed that there were no inside spies encouraging January 6 violence. For them, the deposition of Ray Epps conducted in secret confirmed that no conspiracy existed.

Tucker Carlson smelled a rat. It seemed to him that the federal government was overemphasizing the conspiracy aspect of the Ray Epps controversy.

If Ray Epps did not have orders from authorities unnamed, why was Epps able to avoid federal prosecution?

After all, FBI agents were conducting raids all over the

country and breaking down doors at the homes of citizens who were not even in Washington at the time of the insurrection.

All you had to do was whisper something about the January 6 events and soon a federal task force would be battering down your front door and brandishing weapons in front of your children.

If in fact, Epps encouraged the insurrection independently, then why wasn't he held responsible for those independent efforts? The video clearly shows Ray Epps acted as a ringleader.

The fact that he intended no harm and actually wanted to diffuse the situation is not a defense. January 6 defendants proving the lack of malicious intent are serving stiff sentences for misdemeanor acts as the federal government cracks down on protesters who never acted as ringleaders or provocateurs in the fashion of Ray Epps.

Tucker Carlson made it clear in multiple broadcasts that the Democratic Party's efforts to paper over the Ray Epps crimes didn't eliminate the possibility of a conspiracy. According to Carlson the non-prosecution of Ray Epps increased the likelihood that some nefarious entity operated behind the scenes to create a picture of anarchy and armed rebellion.

Tucker Carlson was relentless in asking these questions, playing the video of Ray Epps urging entry into the Capitol repeatedly on national television in program after program.

He was not going to let go of this matter until the following question was answered in its entirety: why wasn't Ray Epps subject to prosecution?

Tucker Carlson's persistence in this matter was supported through congressional testimony by the FBI. When asked directly by Republicans as to the existence of undercover agents in the January 6 crowd, representatives of the FBI refused to answer the questions.

Tucker Carlson realized that it would be easy to deny participation in the January 6 riots if the nonparticipation were true. Instead, avoidance of the question by federal government witnesses before Congress seem to be pointing to the obvious answer.

Something about the narrative created by the January 6 committee smelled like dead fish. And remember, the carcass of a dead fish rots from the head down, and Tucker Carlson was getting dangerously close to the truth.

But the media machine in the Ray Epps protection program wasn't done yet.

Sixty Minutes, the once highly respected longform news program from the CBS television network went to work. They gave Ray Epps his own featured spot on the Sunday night show.

Epps was given a very sympathetic softball interview on the program in which he claims that Tucker Carlson was ruining his life because of the continued drumbeat coverage by Carlson on a regular basis on the Fox News Channel.

Ray Epps is seen pleading on camera for Carlson to abandon his conspiratorial theories and let Ray Epps live his life in peace as a patriotic citizen and Middle East war veteran.

But Tucker Carlson has and continues to point to the ongoing unanswered question: why was Ray Epps not prosecuted when other less involved individuals with innocent intentions are left to rot away in the squalid jails of Washington DC?

In a world where Democrats promote the elimination of

bail so that defendants can roam free until trial, why are January 6 defendants potentially guilty of nothing more than misdemeanor trespassing with no criminal record incarcerated without even a bail hearing?

Why was Ray Epps left untouched when the Justice Department was determined to drop the boot of the government on the necks of those who barely participated in the controversial events of that fateful day on January 6?

What was the answer to the Ray Epps question?

One man in the media would not let this go. And that man was Tucker Carlson.

In July 2023 there was a new development as Ray Epps filed a lawsuit against Fox News because of the way Carlson hammered away seeking answers to the Ray Epps mystery.

The lawsuit alleges that the Justice Department will indeed prosecute Epps but only because of Carlson's persistent coverage of Epps' activities on January 6.

Carlson is giving no ground when it comes to the Ray Epps situation. He is skeptical of Ray Epps' explanations and is skeptical regarding a potential prosecution as a too-little-too-late attempt to destroy any conspiracy theories.

Carlson asserts that the man who served as the Chief of the Capitol Hill police on January 6 told Carlson directly that federal agents were populated all throughout the "insurrectionist" crowd on that day. Capitol Hill police chief Steven Sund revealed this information in a Carlson interview that preceded Tucker's departure from Fox.

Fox News owns this interview and has chosen not to release it publicly. But Carlson swears that the interview exists and has even threatened to conduct a new interview to get Sund on the record regarding federal agents on January 6.

The truth regarding this matter hopefully will come out eventually and when it does it is likely to come forward because of the efforts of Tucker Carlson.

CHAPTER 34
LINDSEY GRAHAM

The greatest composers of symphonies such as Beethoven, Mozart, and Haydn have created familiar musical sequences that we immediately recognize. The first four notes of Beethoven's Fifth have been so recognizable that commercials use those notes to convey images of importance and grandeur.

So embedded in our psyche are those notes that a disco version of those notes was a big hit in the 1980s.

What people forget about the classical masters is that the great works so well known for their major theme frequently have a minor theme that pops up occasionally throughout the score.

The minor theme may be somewhat less memorable, but nonetheless you can count on it reappearing throughout the symphonic work.

Thus it is with Tucker's criticism of South Carolina Senator Lindsey Graham. Tucker despises him not so much as a RINO (Republican In Name Only) but as a hypocrite, always leading archconservative parades while quietly voting for a leftist agenda.

Tucker says as much and he says it with utter disdain for Senator Graham. The interesting thing here is that Tucker can go weeks without mentioning his name and then devote an entire segment to attack Graham's duplicity.

Unfortunately for Graham, the senator likes to keep himself in the news, so Tucker obliges him with the occasional exposing of Lindsey's fraud as the headlines require.

Sometimes it's just plain weird. Tucker doesn't like Trump's personal traits but he loves Trump's desire to put American interests first.

As others line up to support Trump, there appears Lindsey Graham giving stump speeches for Trump and defending him in the well of the Senate.

But Carlson is not fooled. While Graham dramatically defended Trump's judicial appointments, he helped shepherd a host of ultra-liberal Biden appointments to the federal district and circuit court benches.

Carlson sees Graham as wanting to bask in the ultra-conservative glow of Donald Trump while quietly aligning with the liberal elites running Washington into the ground with unnecessary wars and out-of-control spending.

The hawkish tendencies of Graham outrage Carlson as he sees Graham as very willing to spend American blood and treasure where no clear advantage for America is present.

Trump is tough but opposes senseless military intervention. Graham never met a military expedition he didn't like.

For this reason, it's weird that Trump campaigns with

Graham, but Trump doesn't mind if the South Carolina Senator sponges off the Trump popularity. Trump is a realistic politician.

Tucker on the other hand has no patience with such fake conservatism.

As the Ukrainian war continued to suck American dollars into a black hole, Graham declared himself a bloodthirsty anti-Russian. Trump does not agree, preferring a negotiated peace instead of a war that could lead to a nuclear conflagration.

On the issue of the January 6 "insurrection" Graham told Capitol Hill police to shoot unarmed protesters. Graham vociferously joined Pelosi in mischaracterizing peaceful loiterers as trying to overthrow our government.

Carlson called him out on this saying Graham is Trumps ally only as "a friend of convenience".

Carlson told Republican candidates to make fun of Graham in 2022, Carlson viewing Graham's pseudo-conservatism as a pathway to defeat.

Carlson, who spent weeks on the ground in Iraq observing the failure of the neocon "nation building", attacked Graham as an all-out liar in the form of Graham's optimism related to United States troops in Afghanistan.

Carlson saw that the Russians couldn't bring Afghanistan to heal, and neither could America. Yet Graham smiled as Americans died in pursuit of an unobtainable objective.

Carlson knew that Graham didn't believe this lie, but Carlson knew that the lie was good for Graham's career. The ultimate hypocrite.

Meanwhile the Carlson-Graham divide was diminishing the goodwill between Carlson and his fellow Fox News host

Sean Hannity. Hannity rarely argued with his friends and Graham was a friend.

Graham was and continues to be a frequent Hannity guest, each segment peppered with Graham's support for deployment of United States soldiers and weapons.

Carlson hated that Hannity was helping Graham shill for the military-industrial complex getting rich while Marines died and taxes crippled businesses.

Hannity kept Graham as a regular guest but the "handoff" exchange between Carlson and Hannity as Hannity took over the airwaves at 9 PM began to be chilly.

Carlson regularly challenged Graham to appear with Tucker on his show, but Graham would rather have dental surgery.

In August 2021, Hannity and Carlson had a brief exchange as Hannity took the broadcast baton from Carlson. In the brief repartee, Hannity pretended to be unable to hear Carlson's closing remarks. In those remarks, Carlson called Graham a coward and a liar. Hannity was about to feature Graham on his own program. Hannity smiled, pretending not to hear the attack and then continued with the show.

Graham raised the ire of Carlson on the issue of immigration as well. While Trump wants limited legal immigration enforced by a wall, Graham favors immigration law exceptions that turn our borders into Swiss cheese, allowing big business access to low-wage labor.

Again, Graham said he loves Trump but then opposes trump policies. Carlson hates this.

Carlson will never sit idly by and see Trump compromised by the likes of Graham. But then, why is Graham aligning himself with Trump on the campaign trail.

Carlson has a theory but instead of a summary we reprint here the comments of Tucker Carlson from February 1, 2023:

> Why is Lindsey Graham on stage with a man he disagrees with on everything and apparently doesn't even like? Simple: Lindsey Graham believes that Trump may get the Republican nomination and he is trying to control Donald Trump through flattery. Not through argument or with facts and reason, as you do with adults, but with false praise. These are the politics of the late Ottoman court, transplanted to Washington. Tell the ruler what he wants to hear so that you are free to subvert what the ruler wants. There is nothing uglier or more demeaning to all involved or, by the way, less democratic. There's nothing more sinister than a flatterer. If you have a choice between a man who wants to punch you in the face or a man who is willing to tell you a lie and claim you're great, choose the guy with a cocked fist every time because you are less likely to get hurt.

Tucker is so perturbed by the weasely nature of Senator Lindsey Graham, that he seemed to imply that the South Carolina Senator is a homosexual. During one broadcast he referred to Graham as "the most *flamboyant* neocon in the Senate". Dave Feliciano, one of Graham's competitors in a Republican senatorial primary, once described Graham as "ambiguously gay".

Graham has never been married and this has fueled rumors of his alleged homosexuality, occasionally making Graham the object of crude humor.

Carlson really took Graham to task after sources said that Donald Trump's ill-advised interviews with Bob Woodward of Watergate fame only occurred because Graham directed

Trump to do so. The Woodward interviews were featured in a subsequent Bob Woodward book highly critical of Trump. Carlson basically felt that only a Trump enemy would want Trump to do a sit-down with the Trump-hating Woodward.

Lindsey Graham at the podium with President Trump.

The thing about Carlson is this: if you are straightforward about your left-leaning tendencies, Tucker will disagree with you, but he will respect you.

On the other hand, if you pretend to be something that you are not for the purposes of advancing your own career, Carlson will not only disagree with you, but he won't respect you and he will do everything in his power to expose you.

That's why this little war between Tucker Carlson and Lindsey Graham is likely to continue over the next few years. Carlson is giving no ground in his opposition to Lindsey Graham the liar and it is likely that the current Trump presidential campaign will create ample opportunity for Carlson to broadcast further tirades against the South Carolina Senator.

What's hard to say is who will come out on top in this fracas, especially if Trump continues to recognize Graham as a political ally. One thing is for sure, Carlson will get his jabs in because he truly believes that Graham is no friend of honest patriotic authentic conservatives.

If Trump prevails and becomes president in 2024, will Graham be offered a cabinet post? It's a distinct possibility, but as long as Tucker Carlson has breath in him to broadcast, he will make sure that this does not happen.

Nothing like a good street fight among Republicans.

I'm betting my money on Carlson.

CHAPTER 35
TRUMP PREDICTION

In 2016 Tucker Carlson strayed away from the well-worn path of typical mainstream Republican thinking and broke away into the brush using his pen as a scythe to blaze a brand-new trail as a political commentator.

Institutional Republicans looked at Donald Trump as a joke and refused to take him seriously as a candidate. Pundits dutifully repeated this thinking and laughed out loud at the absurdity of Donald Trump as a serious presidential candidate.

Go to *YouTube* and type in "2016 mocking Trump's candidacy" and you will see video after video of talking heads of the most highly respected commentators making fun of the Donald's presidential ambition. The piling on by mainstream experts showed a near unanimous contempt for Donald Trump as a political figure.

And there certainly were external features of Donald Trump that made him appear to be less than professional as a would-be statesman. His ridiculous haircut. His bombastic rhetoric. His juvenile schoolyard name-calling of opponents. His New York Street fighter vocabulary.

It was obvious to just about everybody in media and government that Donald Trump was a rank amateur unable to ascend into the ranks of professional politicians.

This opinion was more than universal amidst the political intelligentsia. It was a signal of one's moral virtue as a prognosticator of where America was going politically.

To be taken seriously in the media, you had to be a card-carrying member of the Never-Trump Society. Failure to do so meant that you were some kind of anarchist hell-bent on the destruction of the pillars of our society. If you loved your country and you cherished your family, your attitude toward Trump had to be a combination of mocking derision mixed with a little bit of hate. This was the rule of the day in early 2016.

Those who had the temerity to stray from the required rule were mercilessly attacked by audiences and television hosts. If you really want to see some great entertainment, look for the clip of Ann Coulter appearing on a television show called *Real-time* with Bill Maher in 2016.

When the host asked Coulter to predict who will be the Republican candidate, she announces with confidence that Trump will be the winner. The audience's reaction and the reaction of the other panel members is absolutely precious. The derisive laughter from both is not in the category of a slight giggle. The mocking laughter is uproarious in nature and lasts several seconds as Coulter blushes at the over-the-top reaction.

Comedians across the country were envious because none of their jokes elicited such loud peals of laughter. Media hosts and columnists across America played a game called Trump whack-a-mole where it was important for them to slam down any person who gave any credence whatsoever to the idea that Trump was a sincere candidate with an authentic chance of victory.

This is the backdrop for the emergence of Tucker Carlson not only as a prophet of political outcomes but as an analyst providing detailed reasons for his prediction.

In January 2016, Tucker Carlson predicted a Trump victory all the way to the White House.

Carlson firmly proclaiming Trump's future victory really stunned the media world. Carlson was known for his conservative opinions but was also known as being more of an institutional Republican in the vein of a John McCain or George Bush the elder.

Mainstream media had viewed Carlson as a traditional conservative favoring tax cuts and controlled spending. Many disagreed with Carlson, but they always saw him as a good guy with common sense and rational thinking.

Carlson's position on Trump was treated as an outrageous violation of one's moral duty to stick with the players that had been on the team for a long time promoting interests of corporate America. Trump should be treated as an interloper and an outcast never to be admitted into the private club of legitimate presidential aspirants.

The laughable part about this situation was that Tucker Carlson was merely predicting the Trump victory. He was not endorsing Trump or asking anyone to support him.

This didn't matter. The mainstream press vilified Tucker Carlson merely for predicting Trump's victory even if he didn't ask anyone to vote for him.

But Tucker Carlson had committed two sins for which he would never be forgiven.

The first sin was that Carlson's prediction lent a certain degree of legitimacy to the Trump presidential movement. Mainstream thinking held that Trump would never have a chance if the electorate could be convinced that he would never be a serious contender. Voters don't like to throw away their votes on candidates who don't have a meaningful following to begin with.

Low ranking candidates usually end up as footnotes to history like the time that Ralph Nader and Jesse Jackson ran for president. If the media convinces the public that a candidate is not a top-tier candidate, then the low ranking becomes a self-fulfilling prophecy.

In essence, if the media convinces the public that a candidate is a long shot also-ran, that candidate is permanently stuck in the basement while the media embraces candidates standing on the roof of the building basking in the sunlight of popular acclaim.

And here was Tucker Carlson throwing a monkey-wrench into the media's game plan of turning Donald Trump into a political non-entity.

Tucker Carlson was committing the cardinal sin of giving Donald Trump political credibility when he had virtually none.

It's important here to point out that Tucker's prediction didn't just give Trump credibility because of the substance of the prediction. It gave Trump credibility especially because the prediction was coming from Tucker Carlson who was regarded as a very savvy and reliable political analyst. Those on the left may not agree with Tucker's politics but they had to give the devil his due.

Tucker Carlson usually knew what he was talking about when it came to predicting the outcome of the big games.

That's one of the reasons why he was in so much demand on the television cable news circuit and is a speaker at various functions across the country.

Tucker Carlson was no Ann Coulter. He wasn't a bomb thrower. He was an articulate describer of the political landscape, and he backed up his opinions with details and data.

Trump became a serious candidate because Tucker Carlson took him seriously.

Shameful.

Absurd.

Unbelievable.

Foolish.

And pure Tucker.

The second sin in Tucker Carlson's pronouncement of Trump's legitimacy was that Carlson did more than issue a prediction. He specifically listed all the reasons for his prediction and those reasons essentially constituted a detailed intricate indictment of the Republican Party.

It would be one thing for Carlson to foolishly lift up Trump to be on the same level with mainstream candidates like Jeb Bush, Ted Cruz, or Marco Rubio.

But it was quite something else and even a bigger sin than the first for Carlson to back up his prediction with a point-by-point dissection of the Republican Party and its platforms.

Not only was Trump going to win according to Carlson, but he was also going to win because the rest of the Republican Party was wrong when it came to the issues important to the average American citizen.

Carlson described the way in which the Republican Party had essentially fallen into lockstep with the Democratic Party on the issue of immigration. Rich Republicans promoted increased immigration of both the legal and illegal variety as a way of obtaining cheap labor for manufacturing and agriculture.

Democrats also wanted uncontrolled immigration as a way of adding registered Democrats to the voter rolls. Both parties wanted to reap the benefit of open borders especially from the Southwest of the United States. For this reason, both parties saw border enforcement as a negative factor.

Trump distinguished himself with his muscular and sometimes aggressive desire to enforce immigration laws that required lawful entry into our country only at designated regulated ports of entry.

While Democratic and Republican leadership decried the Trump position as racist, the average American saw Trump as the only candidate willing to say the things that Americans have been thinking for years. Americans did not oppose immigration generally, but they did oppose Swiss cheese borders that promoted drug trafficking, sex trafficking, and foreign criminals looking for a way to ply their trade in the United States.

Carlson told the world that Trump was right on this issue and that the country club set sitting atop the Republican Party did not understand the feelings of the average American.

Carlson realized that Trump was saying what the average American was thinking. He may not have been saying it very eloquently and he might've been saying it in a way that was politically incorrect but nonetheless he was saying it. Tucker realized that Trump's statements were hitting the bull's-eye when it came to targeting potential voters from both parties.

Tucker also hit Republicans hard on the issue of NAFTA. Trump attacked NAFTA because he felt this treaty promoted international trade at the cost of American jobs. Carlson realized that Trump was right and that he was the only one loudly attacking this deal that had been promoted by Clinton, Bush the younger, and Obama.

The average union member in America saw NAFTA as an insider deal made to benefit corporations to the detriment of the little guy.

While Republican and Democratic candidates shied away from the issue, Trump told the truth in his own inimitable caustic style. But since Carlson realized that Trump was telling the truth, Carlson took the opportunity to pull the mask away to reveal the ugly self-serving motivations of Republican leadership.

On issue after issue, stated Carlson, Trump was revealing the truth about elite Washington insiders who manipulated the electorate to keep their exclusive money machine going.

Trump really upset the elites when he exposed the cozy relationship between producers of military weapons and government leaders. The Bush administration had full congressional cooperation in an effort to build democracies in countries that preferred theocratic rulers.

Billions of dollars were being wasted and American soldiers were losing their lives in the name of nation building. Trump attacked these policies in favor of an *America First* policy that wanted our tax dollars to help the average American citizen instead of creating wealth for Raytheon and other military providers.

Carlson correctly realized long before anybody else did that United States continued to pursue policies that hurt the average American while lining the pockets of congressmen, senators, and corporate leaders.

This attack by Carlson of the *status quo* in the form of his reasoned explanation for Trump's success really put Carlson on the outs with mainstream Republicans who were now exposed as knowingly hurting the average Joe so that they could get rich.

And the irony of it all did not escape Carlson's attention. He realized that Donald Trump, as a freewheeling wealthy real estate magnate, should be the last person to criticize the monied elite. After all, Trump made millions in his real estate deals while frequently using the bankruptcy laws to escape payment to contractors that had performed for him in good faith.

In other words, Carlson identified Trump as a wealthy elitist unlikely to attack another wealthy elitist.

But Carlson accurately identified that Trump was unique in that he was willing to tell the truth even if it exposed the dark underbelly of high-level American business and political practices. In other words, Trump was willing to reveal corruption and the average American loved it.

The Trump phenomena reminds us of the progressive activism of President Theodore Roosevelt during the early 1900s. Teddy Roosevelt came from a family that used prestige and old money, never suffering deprivation because he was born with a multitude of proverbial silver spoons in his mouth.

Teddy Roosevelt, however, touched a nerve in the American psyche when he went after corporate abuse of the little guy in America. Roosevelt championed reform measures in the areas of corporate collusion, child labor, unsafe food practices, regulation of untested pharmaceuticals, and dangerous work conditions in American factories.

Teddy Roosevelt was popular with the little guy because he was a rich guy that knew all the tricks invented in corporate board rooms. Who would be more qualified to stop corporate abuse than a man who had a front row seat in the creation of those abuses.

This became painfully apparent to Democrats especially when Trump was asked how he justified inviting Hillary Clinton to his daughter's wedding if he had such a low opinion of Hillary Clinton. Trump did not hesitate to answer this question that was presented to him on the debate stage. He immediately responded by announcing that he had *paid* Hillary Clinton to attend the wedding.

Here was a very wealthy man revealing the way in which he used his power and wealth to get high profile personalities to attend his daughter's wedding.

Trump was willing to admit that he himself used power to manipulate people even if only to impress others by getting a bunch of A-listers onto the guest list for his daughter's wedding reception. Even in relation to something as personal as his daughter's wedding, Trump the powerbroker reduced his every move to another way to enhance his own profile in the business and political world.

He was shameless in this regard but also stunningly honest. Americans loved this kind of bold candor and they realized that they saw in Trump a brand-new kind of politician. A powerful truth teller who just didn't give a crap about what anyone else thought. Americans like this.

That was how Donald Trump came across and Tucker saw this.

In making his prediction of Trump success, Carlson did not hide his contempt for Trump's rudeness and boorish style.

He felt that in many ways Donald Trump was a disgusting vulgar buffoon with a poor attitude toward women and an insulting vocabulary that would lead to a certainly inelegant if not embarrassing presidency.

Carlson blamed the Republican Party and the mainstream media for creating Trump and for ignoring the issues that Americans truly cared about and that were front and center in Trump's campaign.

The most important thing about Carlson's approach to Trump is that it marked a sea change when it came to the media's perception of Carlson. In some ways, Carlson was showing the same kind of reckless courage that Trump was showing as Carlson predicted Trump's victory and explained the reasons behind it.

It was clear that Carlson was now his own man. He wasn't taking orders from anybody including Donald Trump. He was trying to be the umpire that makes the calls as he sees them, even if it subjected him to cancellation of his membership in the good old boys' club.

The entire Trump candidacy revealed something about Carlson that would endear him to the American public as time marched forward.

Tucker Carlson now could be accurately described as something that would ultimately lead to greater success in his career.

Independent.

CHAPTER 36
LIFE

That Tucker Carlson's view of the world certainly has evolved over the years is obvious, but he remains principled and clearly attached to the advancement of his core values.

His criticism of the military-industrial complex cashing in on bipartisan support for the Ukraine war is a far cry from his support of Bush style Republicans preceding his eye-opening experiences in Iraq. That incident clearly changed him as he realized that the Neocons and Democrats joined forces to line the pockets of defense contractors and politicians frequently at the expense of American lives.

But this recalibration of his view of our government leaders did not impact his stalwart allegiance to his central beliefs.

Nowhere is this more clear than looking at his stand on abortion. Carlson has always been unabashedly pro-life and in some ways this is surprising.

Carlson developed his political philosophy mostly based

on the ideas of a free-market economy and capitalism. In other words, Carlson usually projected himself as more of an economic conservative rather than being a cultural conservative.

Abortion however, is an area in which Carlson has without hesitation or compromise stood on the side of protecting the lives of unborn children.

It is also of great interest that he takes this position against abortion when this position contrasts with the teachings of the Episcopal Church.

Carlson over the years has proudly proclaimed that he is a regular churchgoer, a faithful Episcopalian practitioner.

Despite this, Carlson is a vocal defender of the unborn child in the face of the Episcopalian Church's official proclamation that women should have the right to choose termination of a pregnancy if they so desire.

Dedicated Episcopalian Tucker Carlson refuses to give ground on the issue of abortion regardless of the position of church fathers in the Episcopalian religion.

Carlson's ardent defense of the unborn goes back many years.

He wrote about this extensively in the *Weekly Standard* in December of 1996.

The article showed that abortions increased as the testing for Down's Syndrome during pregnancy increased. Carlson traces the advances of medical researchers as the Down's Syndrome test evolved from *amniocentesis* to a simple and relatively convenient blood test.

He shows clearly that American women were choosing abortion because the now noninvasive testing process allowed them to avoid giving birth to a Down's Syndrome child. In fact, he demonstrates with statistical certainty that women choose abortion most frequently as an avoidance of the Down's Syndrome baby.

Carlson is horrified and describes this development as a form of Nazi style eugenics first encouraged by Margaret Sanger as one of the core principles of Planned Parenthood. Sanger along with her follower Adolf Hitler essentially sought purification of humanity through the murder of unborn children undesirable in the eyes of aristocrats.

Carlson even details the ways in which the scientists who developed the Down's Syndrome testing process were filled with regret because the test has led to the genocide of millions of unborn babies. The testing, according to its inventor, was designed to help women and families prepare to care for these children, not to lead to death in the womb.

The most striking thing about this article is the time Carlson spends describing the blessings bestowed upon the families with the Down's Syndrome child. Carlson relates stories of tender love and joy surrounding these kids. He describes Down's Syndrome families living life to the fullest because of a child who brings out the best in all the members of the family.

Is there extra sacrifice involved? Yes.

Are there some limitations? Yes.

But the Tucker Carlson story printed in *The Weekly Standard* conveys a sense of the divine seen in these special children and the ways in which these loving families reflect that divinity in the form of unfiltered love.

The piece is moving and leaves the reader ashamed about the mere thought of ending an innocent life. Carlson tells us that these sweet lovable Down's Syndrome children are worth protecting even if caring for them is sometimes difficult and expensive.

You come away from the Carlson submission recognizing the preciousness of life and the sheer evil that is part of the pro-abortion philosophy.

Carlson once wrote that he was amazed by the manic over-the- top animal-rights activists who would stop at nothing to eliminate fur coats but would willingly go along with the idea that the innocent child in the womb did not deserve protection. Said Carlson in 2003, "I've never met an animal rights activist who wasn't strongly in favor of abortion for people."

Carlson's absolute dedication to the protection of little babies was clarified in his now famous interview with Monica Klein on the Fox News *Tucker Carlson Tonight* Show in 2019.

Let me set the scene for you. Virginia Governor Ralph Northam had just completed a video interview in which he indicated that a newborn baby should be left to die after an abortion attempt failed to end the pregnancy.

This video went viral as moralists both Democrat and Republican were shocked to hear that a politician sided with the concept of infanticide.

As you'd expect, pro-life organizations promoted distribution of the video as a demonstration of the callous disregard for human life that lay at the heart of the pro-abortion philosophy.

Carlson played the video multiple times on his own TV show but in fairness also invited a pro-abortion political operative to make an appearance. Monica Klein was a Democrat party consultant formerly a member of the administration of Mayor Bill De Blasio in New York City.

During the interview, Carlson challenged Klein, asking if she agreed that it was morally improper to kill a baby born alive despite a failed abortion attempt. Klein deflected and refused to answer.

Carlson came back to that very same basic question again and again. Did Monica Klein and her pro-abortion cohorts accept the idea that it was moral and proper to end the life of a newborn child after a failed abortion?

No matter how many times Carlson raised the question, Klein refused to respond to it, instead robotically reverting to pro-abortion talking points involving freedom of choice for the mother.

Klein finally started getting angry, telling Carlson that men had no right to tell a woman what to do with her body. Carlson responded by asking her why she didn't care about the baby's body.

Now Klein was really agitated, but she refused to answer the question. She had to know it was coming because of the Virginia governor's video that was the topic of conversation all over America.

The interview ended with Carlson exasperated because the guest would not answer the question. Monica Klein was frustrated because she failed to get "Pitbull" Carlson to move the discussion in the direction of the pro-abortion talking points.

But if anyone had any questions about Tucker Carlson's pro-life *bona fides*, those questions were put to rest after that interview.

Tucker Carlson really threw down the gauntlet in February 2023 after watching President Biden's State of the Union Speech. During the speech, several Democratic politicians including Congresswoman Alexandria Ocasio-Cortez and Senator Ed Markey were wearing pins promoting abortion in which the letter "o" in the word "abortion" was reproduced in the shape of a heart. The clear message was that they "loved" abortion.

Tucker Carlson immediately went on the air and delivered a scathing commentary in which he asked the world how it could be possible that any human being could say that they "loved" human sacrifice.

The "I love abortion" pin was worn by Senator Ed Markey at the 2023 State of The Union Address. Carlson was outraged.

That's right, he called abortion human sacrifice.

The evil of human sacrifice, which had been an obscene religious practice through the centuries, was, according to Carlson, alive and well in the cold practice of abortion. The spilling of the blood of millions of innocent children was now being affectionately justified on the lapels of American politicians.

Despite the attacks on Carlson for his identification of abortion as human sacrifice, Carlson did not back down in what was now clearly one of Carlson's crusades.

Carlson's dynamic defense of the unborn reached a

crescendo as he delivered his last major public address to the *Heritage Foundation* on April 26, 2023.

In the speech, he again described abortion as a despicable form of human sacrifice leading to the homicide of millions of children. However, he also specifically attacked President Biden's Treasury Secretary Janet Yellen. Just a year prior to the Heritage Foundation speech, Yellen appeared at a hearing before the United States Senate.

Senator Robert Menendez asked how abortion rights affected the economy in general.

Yellen seemed to be reading from a prepared text as she told the senator that elimination of abortion rights would have an extremely detrimental impact on the economy. She elaborated that women must have the right to murder their children in the womb to more fully participate in the job market. The Treasury Secretary said that eliminating abortion would constitute a serious barrier to labor force participation. She went on further to say that this barrier to labor force participation would hurt the "well-being of children".

Carlson used the Heritage Foundation speech to expose the Democratic Party hypocrisy when it comes to children. The video from the speech shows a Tucker Carlson highly agitated and even emotional because government officials would rather sacrifice unborn children than experience any kind of economic discomfort.

This presentation is really the high watermark demonstrating Carlson's unflinching desire to rescue unborn children from the abortionist's deadly scalpel.

The *Heritage Foundation* talk concludes with one additional poignant moment. Carlson ends by imploring the audience to ask God to rescue us from the evils penetrating every aspect of our culture. Carlson was overcome with emotion, contemplating the modern holocaust of abortion.

Without doubt, as Tucker Carlson's career with Fox News was heading over the cliff, Tucker Carlson's desire to save unborn children was at its zenith.

CHAPTER 37
WHY HE FIGHTS

In 2022 Tucker Carlson conducted one of his longform interviews for broadcast carried on a Fox subsidiary streaming service called *Fox Nation*. The longform program was titled *Tucker Carlson Today* and it truly allowed Carlson to plunge the depths of subjects too complex to be properly illuminated on Tucker's nightly Fox news channel program.

The interview I'm writing about now is important because it allows Carlson fans to understand what drives Carlson in the pursuit and proclamation of truth.

Here's what happened. Carlson in this program featured a guest by the name of Mattias Desmet. Desmet is a Belgian doctor of psychology who has studied and written extensively about a subject known as ***mass formation***.

Mass formation is the name for the phenomena of entire populations blindly embracing counterproductive actions in an almost unanimous fashion.

Dr. Desmet holds up the examples of the communist revolution in Russia and the Nazi takeover of Germany in the 1930s.

In both instances, powerful evil leadership engaged in a form of hypnotic persuasion that rendered entire nations incapable of opposing government narratives that were not only lies but were also harmful to the citizens themselves. Mass formation is an exercise of raw power that inspires slavish adherence to government directives by convincing people that opposition to the government directive would be a violation of the social contract between citizens.

Mass formation is so powerful that it causes people to override their very deepest held personal values.

This is the reason that Russians believed Stalin's propaganda and accepted his murderous methods. The population was so swept up in the fever of Stalin's Marxism that they were willing to suspend all the moral concepts of their religion and their families.

Likewise, Hitler and his propagandists thoroughly used mass formation to penetrate the hearts of otherwise intelligent compassionate people. The elimination of the Jews became an objective that unified the German people so completely that it seemed an absurdity to oppose the Third Reich.

It is obviously a frightening concept. Carlson's guest from Belgium described an instance in the Iranian revolution against the Shah in which a mother turned her own son into the police because he had spoken out against the Ayatollah. She personally placed the hangman's noose around her son's neck, completely taken in by the mass formation project imposed on Iranian citizens.

It's hard to imagine.

There's more.

The professor then details the way that mass formation

had occurred during the Covid lockdowns in America. The Belgian expert explained that intense social pressure allowed Americans to hurt themselves and their families in the name of social compliance.

The actual scientific data did not support the use of extreme measures in the form of forced vaccinations. This didn't matter because the influence of mass formation would override logic and truth.

The Belgian was shocked that Americans cooperated when grandparents were forced to spend their final days alone and without family in infected nursing homes. Only the psychological grip of mass formation, said the Belgian, could override the human desire to be with loved ones in the final moments of life.

The government-issued Corona orders destroyed families and businesses and were completely unsupported by the actual science that was censored by the government and its partners in big tech and mass media.

Those who opposed the orders were depicted as criminals. Dr. Desmet told Carlson that the similarities between the lockdowns and the Nazi era were chilling.

The lockdowns, explained the doctor, were the result of mass formation growing out of a blind attachment to the scientific pronouncements of a chosen few.

This meant that those people with a contrasting scientific view or even those armed with data proving the government was lying had to be ostracized and driven out of proper society because they were unwilling to cooperate in the objectives of the mass formation lie.

Dr. Desmet described what happened in America during the lockdowns as *technocratic totalitarianism*.

He also told Carlson that his theories were not new ones. A German academician named Hannah Arendt developed this line of thought in the 1930s as Hitler and his goons were using violence to create a unity of thought in Germany.

Arendt escaped Germany before the dark shadow of Nazism seized control of that country. She became an important author as she explained the way that mass transformation is at the heart of totalitarian rule.

Dr. Mattias Desmet told Tucker that fighting for the truth could save civilization.

The final stages of mass formation, warned Dr. Desmet, manifested themselves in the form of intimidating violence and ultimately death camps for the noncompliant.

Tucker Carlson was truly moved by this interview.

Carlson had just one more question before they turned off the cameras.

He wanted the good doctor to explain what could be done to stop mass formation so that it could never evolve into the stage of violence and deprivation.

Desmet explained that the key was to stop mass formation in its early stages through *a willingness to stand up and tell the truth.*

Dr. Desmet realized that as mass formation takes root, a small contingent of the population, usually around 5% of the whole, have a clear understanding of the truth.

The phenomena of mass formation, with its potential to conclude with executions and tortures, could be stopped in its infant stages if brave citizens were willing to proclaim the truth before the lies have the opportunity to turn all of us into bloodthirsty zombies.

You can find this interview on *YouTube* and you must see it. You can see that a light goes off inside the soul of Tucker Carlson as he realizes that his pursuit of truth in the face of governmental and corporate propaganda is more than his effort to be a good newsman.

He realizes that pursuit of truth at all costs can act as a barrier against mass formation. Without the Tucker Carlsons of the world opposing government fictions, those fictions are free to develop into evil policies embraced by the hypnotized populace.

The French Revolution led to the execution of protesters while the rest of French citizens idly encouraged a death sentence for nonbelievers.

Hitler's propaganda minister Joseph Goebbels felt that the bigger the lie the easier it is to sell to the population on a mass level.

Tucker Carlson was overcome by the sober thought that he was now saddled with the responsibility of getting the truth out there not for the purpose of good ratings or for the purpose of supporting his favorite politicians.

Tucker Carlson now realized that the American concepts of freedom, self-determination, and peace were in danger without truth-telling to interrupt the mass formation cycle.

And this is why Tucker Carlson fights for the truth. And this is why all of us must join him in this effort. The greatest nation in the history of the world is in danger of collapsing in the face of mass formation made possible by the threat of technocratic totalitarianism.

The Tucker Carlson solution is the solution for every

American. Fight hard to find the truth and fight even harder to make sure that it gets out to the world.

On a personal level, Tucker Carlson has great wealth and all of us know that wealth can buy an awful lot of freedom. But he knows that his personal wealth is not enough to save the freedom of his countrymen.

And that's why he fights.

He's a tough Mother Tucker!

CHAPTER 38
ANOTHER CARLSON FIRED

Nobody knows who said it first but it's one of the axioms in major league baseball that managers are hired to be fired. Billy Martin understood this in the 1980s as he guided the New York Yankees to various championships and into the World Series on numerous occasions.

The thing was, he was always getting fired, and then hired, and then fired again. During one 10-year period George Steinbrenner hired Billy Martin to be the manager of the New York Yankees five separate times only to fire him eventually each time. It's some kind of record for a single franchise but it emphasizes the idea that in some professions you are only around long enough for your bosses to want to get rid of you.

High-stakes television broadcasting is no different. Tucker Carlson learned this lesson as a kid watching his father fawned over by network executives only to be ignominiously relieved of duty at the drop of a hat.

Richard Carlson, Tucker's father, liked the idea that his son Tucker could see that the highest perch in the media world was a very precarious spot. You could be knocked off at a moment's notice.

Frank Sinatra had a huge hit in 1966 called *That's Life*. The lyric talks about "riding high in April and getting shot down in May".

Richard Carlson used to warn his boys to keep their ego in check, success being a very fleeting commodity.

Tucker Carlson understood all of this only too well. In his career he quickly went from being a modest essay writer to becoming a TV personality shuffled from one production to another and from one cable network to another.

It seems that you are only as good as your last gig. Most importantly, regardless of the gig, television executives tended to be pretty fickle.

The host producers loved on Monday became the host that producers hated on Friday. Let's just say that Tucker Carlson was aware that television was a very "fluid" business.

However, Carson's tenure at the Fox news channel with his production of *Tucker Carlson Tonight* seemed to be the kind of production that would last for the long haul.

Tucker Carlson, already a seasoned performer at only age 46, sat comfortably in the cockpit of the highflying 8 o'clock time slot on the Fox news channel right from the beginning.

It didn't take long for Carlson to hit his stride and it didn't take long for him to amass a huge viewing audience that surpassed the numbers even of the great Bill O'Reilly.

Thereafter ensued year after year with Tucker Carlson as the most-watched television news program in the world, cable or broadcast.

He developed his own style and the ability to break news

stories somehow missed by others, even his colleagues at the Fox News Channel.

Tucker Carlson became the powerhouse engine that drove the Fox News Channel, becoming a moneymaking juggernaut.

Despite all this, Carlson remembered the lessons from his father and although surprised, he realized that the phone call from the Fox executive was real and that his time with Fox was at an end.

The date was April 21, 2023 and he had completed his Friday broadcast on a high note, encouraging viewers to tune in again on Monday evening for another edition of *Tucker Carlson Tonight*.

Carlson then went into his normal weekend routine where he read reports from his research team and began creating a tentative schedule of topics to be covered in the ensuing week.

Every show began with one of Tucker's trademark monologues, always painstakingly written by Carlson himself to deliver maximum impact with reference to a major story. This was Tucker Carlson at his best where his writing skills gave him the opportunity to frequently deliver a world changing speech to America during the first seven minutes of each broadcast.

Sitting at his kitchen table at his home in Maine, his reverie was interrupted by the phone call from one of the Fox network executives. No details were given but the executive told Carlson that the networking decided "to go in another direction". Carlson chuckled to himself a little as the "going in another direction" excuse had become a cliché in a business where executives were rarely honest with their subordinates.

A lot of things raced through his mind as he searched for a reason. Fox had recently coughed up three quarters of a billion dollars to the *Dominion Voting Machine Company* settling a nasty defamation lawsuit.

Carlson also realized that he had been the least culpable of the Fox News Channel hosts who attacked *Dominion* on the air. In fact, Carlson had famously grown impatient with *Dominion* detractors who consistently failed to produce evidence of *Dominion* wrongdoing.

Surprisingly, the phone call was short as the executive told Carlson that there would be no show on Monday or any day thereafter. Carlson was done at Fox News.

The executive admitted that Carlson was still in possession of an unexpired contract. The executive told Carlson that Fox lawyers would reach out to Carlson's lawyers to iron out the details. The executive wanted to get off the phone, having accomplished his nasty mission of ending the Carlson-Fox News partnership.

Carlson immediately told his wife and then contacted his father and the rest of his inner circle.

It had been a great run.

And most importantly, Carlson realized that he still had plenty to say and he began planning alternate routes into the hearts of Americans.

But what was the truth about what actually happened between Tucker Carlson and Fox news?

It's likely that no one will ever learn the real answer because as Tucker Carlson moves forward with his broadcast life, he and Fox News are involved in very intense negotiations to clarify the rights of each side in the post-Tucker Fox News era.

In all likelihood, the parties will settle on terms that will offer one of two options in terms of an explanation.

The first option is no explanation at all with the parties entering into a nondisclosure and confidentiality agreement.

The second option is that the parties will tell the public that they both determined that it was in their mutual interest to part company. No further comment forthcoming.

Obviously, Carlson's main goal is to be left with complete freedom to continue his role as the voice of conservative America.

The Fox News Channel really wants to control the damage to its image and acted quickly to find an effective Tucker Carlson replacement. Unfortunately for Fox News, Carlson was such an unusual commodity that an effective replacement was not obvious.

Fox News recently announced that the 8 o'clock segment will be turned over to Jesse Watters who had been broadcasting at 7 PM as a lead-in to Tucker. The situation is similar to when Tucker took over for O'Reilly. Jesse Watters is about the same age as had been Tucker when he moved into the prime-time spot. Watters is also dynamic and aggressive like Tucker but time will tell if he can reach the Carlson level of success.

This writer also finds it odd that the Fox News Corporation has been so aggressive in its unfriendliness toward Tucker since his departure. Fox News has years of archived videotapes of Tucker Carlson outtakes that shows Carlson when he is not at his finest.

That's why they're called outtakes, never intended to be seen by the public. Fox has discreetly leaked these outtakes to other networks in an effort to diminish Carlson's value in the public eye. This has not been very effective because the outtakes don't reveal much more than a news personality in casual conversation off-camera. Carlson says a couple of vaguely offensive remarks but nothing very much out of the ordinary.

Very surprising has been the pettiness of the Fox position. Rupert Murdoch sent his minions to the special broadcast studio located at Tucker's residence in Maine. Fox News had constructed a beautiful broadcast studio inside a barn located on the Carlson estate. A few weeks after Tucker was dismissed, Murdoch sent contractors and technicians to remove all of the Fox-owned equipment.

Given the high stakes involved in the ongoing settlement negotiations, Fox would've been well advised to hold off on such drastic action. There's no doubt that Fox is entitled to the equipment that they removed, but why aggravate the person with whom you are trying to settle?

It's somewhat mysterious but some speculated that Rupert Murdoch and his children who run the Fox News empire became angry with Tucker Carlson for a few different reasons.

First of all, the Murdoch's were still a little sore about Carlson's broadcast of the January 6 videos. Carlson had made the deal for speaker McCarthy to hand over the tapes without approval from Rupert Murdoch in London.

Murdoch likely would've been okay with it but the fact that Carlson did not even consult with the media mogul rankled him. Murdoch also realized that Carlson was planning future programs releasing even more of the extensive video for public viewing. This got under Murdoch's skin because he just felt he had no editorial control over program content with Tucker Carlson.

Of course, Murdoch was right in the sense that Carlson's

popularity had been converted into media power few could challenge. Carlson through his success had become the most important person in the Murdoch empire.

Murdoch always felt that the most important person in the Murdoch empire should be Murdoch.

Secondly, the Dominion lawsuit made the Murdoch family more sensitive concerning potential defamation lawsuits and the *60 Minutes* interview with Ray Epps gave them a bad feeling that Epps was preparing to sue, which he did eventually.

Executives at Fox had hinted to Carlson that maybe he should back away from any more programs related to Epps as a way of protecting the network from another lawsuit.

Carlson, ever the broadcaster of integrity, did not like this idea, especially since Carlson knew he was telling the truth and especially since Carlson very carefully chose his words in every broadcast to make sure he was not committing slander.

Carlson told the bosses at Fox News Channel to stop worrying because a seasoned professional was not going to do anything stupid. Murdoch wasn't satisfied.

There is one last theory for the source of the Carlson firing that has been reported in print and video by a number of sources. This theory should be given some degree of credence because it has been reported by Chadwick Moore who is the author of a new biography about Tucker Carlson being released in the summer of 2023.

The report from Moore indicates that Carlson was let go as an added promise to *Dominion Voting Machines* as a condition for the settlement of the *Dominion* lawsuit.

Both Fox and *Dominion* deny this. However, Moore claims that he has independent sources in the Fox News hierarchy confirming the story.

What's really weird about this is that Chadwick Moore does not indicate that Carlson himself was aware of such a deal. Carlson may have been kept in the dark but it seems unlikely even though Carlson was not a named party in the original *Dominion* lawsuit. It is unlikely that we will ever know the truth.

Visitors to New York City won't see this banner on the Fox building again.

In the meantime, Tucker Carlson has already made his maiden voyage on Twitter with a program called *Tucker Carlson on Twitter*. His streamed broadcast has the same look and feel of the original *Tucker Carlson Tonight* that was featured on Fox news.

It is, however, an entirely new program that features Tucker Carlson doing the thing that he always does in the form of breaking stories and offering commentary. It truly seems that not even his departure from Fox News will slow him down. Fox is discovering that the internet has created new platforms with the potential to far outstrip the reach even of the mighty and powerful Fox News.

As the presidential elections of 2024 bear down on us, Tucker Carlson is the most important figure in political commentary, and will undoubtedly play an important role in shaping opinions and in influencing the outcome of this important election.

To those of us who have followed his spectacular rise to the top of broadcast journalism, we are glad that Tucker Carlson landed on his feet and we will faithfully follow his reporting and listen to his opinion. The powerful elites who run the world are faced with an unstoppable counterbalance.

His name is Tucker Carlson, one *Tough Mother Tucker.*

CHAPTER 39
TRUMP CARD

Despite Carlson's departure from Fox News for nightly broadcast, Tucker Carlson has hardly faded away. In fact, his "broadcasts" on Twitter are garnering audiences much larger than when he was doing the cable TV news show.

For this reason, Tucker will play an enormous role in shaping public opinion in the upcoming presidential election of 2024.

People want to know which candidate will be backed by Carlson. It's clear that Carlson will have a meaningful impact by simply looking at the past. There are very few in media or politics who believe that J.D. Vance would've been elected to the United States Senate from Ohio without Carlson's unwavering broadcast support.

Now with Carlson commanding an even larger audience and with a following that is arguably even more loyal, Carlson very well could play the role of kingmaker in the upcoming presidential sweepstakes.

Everyone says it is a mystery and that we must wait until

the Republican primary season is underway to determine the nominee from the GOP. It's highly unlikely that given Carlson's pro-life anti-big tech philosophy that Carlson would stand behind the nominee of the Democratic Party.

For this reason, it's clear that Carlson will be stomping for the Republican in the race.

The real question that people ask is whether Carlson will wholeheartedly get behind a Donald Trump candidacy if Trump wins the nomination.

This writer believes that it is obvious and clear that Carlson will dynamically support Trump if he is the Republican nominee.

Here is an explanation of my theory.

Carlson has become a substance over form kind of man over the last several years.

There was a time when the external elements of a candidate could be off-putting for Carlson. Candidates could say strange things or elicit plans that seemed off kilter. Carlson would then stop taking that candidate seriously and gravitate toward a more centrist traditional personality.

But as I have demonstrated in this book, Carlson was deeply changed by his experiences in Iraq. He realized that the ruling elites with all their proper manners and soaring vocabulary were actually liars pursuing their own objectives usually inconsistent with the wishes of the average American citizen.

From that point on, Carlson would pursue the truth and would judge leaders not by what they said but by what they actually did.

And then Donald Trump was elected in 2016.

Carlson repeatedly told the world that Trump's selection was a reaction to leaders from both parties who talked a good game but ignored the American people when it came to action.

And then after he was elected, Donald Trump did an amazing thing.

He actually carried out the wishes of the electorate.

Shocking.

Surprising.

And from that point forward, Carlson was hooked on Trump not because of who Trump was on a personal basis but hooked on Trump because he actually put into practice good policies as he had been instructed by the American people.

The old Clinton-Bush-Obama-Biden crowd delivered soaring speeches about the nobility of diversity while screwing the American middle class with hyperinflation and lockdowns that kept them out of churches.

Trump on the other hand was rude and bombastic but told the truth about the way NAFTA was ruining the life of factory workers. Trump made sexually demeaning cracks about women but told the nation that open borders meant that we really didn't have a nation at all.

Every other national politician promised to move the United States Embassy to Jerusalem but Trump was the only one to actually keep that promise.

Trump refused to be held hostage to climate hustlers and made America energy independent for the first time in years. Trump never lived a good Christian life, but he kept his promise to create a Supreme Court that would protect unborn children.

You see, Carlson is drawn to Trump because Trump tells it like it is just like Carlson tells it like it is. Trump lacks the sophistication and elegance of a Tucker Carlson. But when you cut through all the noise, Carlson loves Trump because

Trump hears the middle-of-America citizen and takes action.

Carlson knows that Trump is more than rough around the edges, that Trump can be a ridiculous jerk that you might not want over to your house to meet your family.

But Carlson saw that Trump could instinctively understand the dreams and complaints of the average Joe. And given Carlson's observation of the *Ship Of Fools* steering our ship of state into one storm after another, he realized that our country needed a leader like Trump, warts and all.

Make no mistake, however, Carlson is truly motivated by his desire to do what is best for America and its citizens. If DeSantis or someone else is the Republican nominee, Carlson will support that person as the best alternative for our country.

That doesn't mean he never liked Trump to begin with. It merely means that Carlson wants good things for good people and will support candidates that actually listen to the electorate.

It's true by the way that Trump continuously says things that confound his own supporters including Carlson.

You can't blame Carlson for the text messages that were revealed as part of the discovery in the *Dominion* election machine litigation. Those revealed text messages showed an emotional Carlson talking about how intensely he hates Trump.

But that hasn't changed the way Carlson is drawn to Trump because Trump tells the truth about the ruling elite the same way that Carlson has attempted to do ever since his Iraqi war experience.

*The love-hate relationship is mostly love: Carlson at a golf
tournament with The Donald.*

The relationship between Trump and Carlson can be
described in the following way: two friends that hate each
other's personal habits but deep down they are kindred
spirits sharing basic values such as standing up to bullies and
protecting the traditional American family.

It's as if Carlson hates nail biting and his best friend in the
world is a notorious nailbiter. Carlson knows that the
disgusting nailbiter will fight to protect his children from
transgender groomers shipping American jobs to China.
Trump doesn't think he needs to attend church services, but
he wants to protect the rights of those who do.

This is not to say that Carlson will campaign for Trump or
the eventual Republican nominee. However, it is clear that
Carlson feels a moral obligation to use his platform as a
weapon in furtherance of honest government.

CHAPTER 40
CORNERSTONE

I n October 2018 Tucker Carlson reached a clarifying moment, almost an epiphany if you will.

He had seen elitists from both parties attempt to suffocate free speech and to diminish the value of objective truth.

As he toured the nation in promotion of his new book *Ship Of Fools*, he found himself with an invitation to speak to the congregation of *The Cornerstone Nashville Assembly of God Church*.

Carlson considered the invitation and said yes. Carlson, a devout practicing Episcopalian, had just agreed to bear his soul in front of an evangelical church.

It's not the sort of thing you would normally do on a book tour, but Carlson did not see the speaking opportunity as a book sales event. He looked at it as an opportunity to examine his own heart and to discuss the soul of America in front of a large crowd of devoted Christians who gladly wore their religion on their sleeves.

Episcopalians are normally a pretty reserved bunch with services that feature quiet prayer and introverted faith. You never hear someone shout "amen!" or "give me a witness!" in a proper Episcopal service.

Therefore, with some trepidation Carlson stepped forward to the pulpit at *Cornerstone* because he realized that the divide in America is not based on party or ideology and wasn't about faith versus science or even reason versus religion but rather was based on theology.

He told the crowd that he had only recently come to the conclusion that the differences in America were theological because it involves those who believe humans are in charge of the universe versus those who believe God is in charge of the universe.

He cited a couple of examples.

If you believed that mankind possessed all power, then humans could declare that a boy could become a girl and that a woman could become a man. If you believed that God was in charge, then the immutable characteristics of the two sexes were controlled by the great deity, our Lord.

On another subject, if you believed in abortion, you believed that you yourself are God with the power to take a life. If you opposed abortion, it was because you accepted that you are not in charge of the universe and that only God has the right to take a life except in the case of self-defense.

Carlson realized that this theological rift grew out of your belief about who actually had power over the universe.

Nonbelieving elitists would never be willing to admit that they were without power and therefore they were forced to adhere to the idea that they were God, the God who could manipulate sex and gender and the God with the authority to snuff out a life struggling for development in the womb.

It was a striking declaration by the talking head who was the hero of patriots throughout America.

Most importantly, the *Cornerstone Church* sermon delivered by Carlson told us everything he believed in context of the big picture.

Carlson, like all of us arguing the issues of the day back and forth over these many years, had really been participating in a question about the exercise of complete power. In other words, everything devolved to whether or not we were willing to submit to the omnipotent power of God or whether we were willing to buy into the false construct that we as humans are in charge.

Carlson's talk at Cornerstone Church ushered in a new era of focus for the news host.

He told the congregation to view our differences through this theological lens in order to find the truth of things. We were made for submission to God, accepting reality, and embracing the joy of forgiveness and ultimately our resurrection.

The talk was joyful and uplifting and eye-opening for

everyone involved and especially for Tucker Carlson himself.

From that point forward, Carlson became more than a talkshow host. Maybe unwittingly and maybe even unwillingly, Carlson emerged from the *Cornerstone Church* as someone in the media who now looked into the camera and offered his commentary on news or politics with a new purpose.

Carlson still did his normal bang-up job of defending freedom and American exceptionalism but now he did it in the context of a clear moral purpose. It was indeed theological, and Tucker Carlson knows who is in charge of the universe.

Carlson is in great demand on the lecture circuit and in his last address delivered prior to his dismissal from Fox, Carlson did something unusual in terms of his giving marching orders to his audience. He didn't tell them how to vote and he didn't tell them to join myriad protest movements.

He told the audience to pray.

He told them to pray for our nation and the future of its people.

While this might be unusual for a political commentator it was not now unusual for Carlson.

He was a new man.

He realized that the theological battle over who is in charge of the universe is so important that it was time to ask for God's help.

This newfound clarity serves as a solid backbone for each broadcast no matter the platform he is utilizing.

We are a great country blessed by the creator and we will survive all her trials because we truly know who is in charge.

This Episcopalian who had heretofore kept his religious

views between himself and his family was recognizing that too much was at stake for the future of our world .

He had a moral obligation to step up and fight the theological battle for our American soul and culture.

This was a completely different Tucker Carlson than the one who delighted in good writing on the various topics of the day. He was no longer an observer of the human pageant.

It has dawned on him that he has a responsibility to preserve the values of self-determination and freedom because powerful forces of evil are hard at work to destroy them.

Carlson deeply loves his children and he has been hit with the reality that his offspring may have to face a Dystopian world of hate and materialism. A world where love, kindness, and respect for others is obliterated in favor of worship of the state above all else.

His conscience won't allow him to take a paycheck in return for a column or a video editorial compromising the truth. Things have gone too far for that.

So in his own way, he is fighting for truth and freedom before it is too late.

This new Tucker Carson is therefore now a warrior. And we need him now more than ever.

We need this *Tough Mother Tucker, America's Truth Warrior.*

CHAPTER 41
EPILOGUE: OUTFOXING
THE FOX

I t is unfortunate that the Fox News Corporation has taken a decidedly adversarial attitude toward Tucker Carlson since concluding Carlson's broadcast opportunities at Fox. When giants part company, frequently the best post-relationship demeanor is for the giants to stay out of each other's way going forward. That way, no one is a victim of the weapons that remain in each giant's arsenal.

For some odd reason, Fox News has ignored this sensible peaceful coexistence posture and has instead tweaked the nose of Tucker Carlson.

As outlined earlier in this book, Fox has tried to diminish Carlson's reputation by releasing somewhat embarrassing out-takes kept in the vault somewhere at Fox headquarters for the sole purpose of seeking retribution against their own television personalities should it become necessary.

The whole thing reveals a pettiness in the Fox News Corporation management and now it's beginning to backfire.

As mentioned in Chapter 34, Tucker Carlson completed a Fox News interview shortly before his discharge. The interview was with the Capitol Hill Police Chief Steven Sund who provided details surrounding the events of January 6, 2021.

No person on earth is more qualified to talk about the so-called "insurrection" than this man who was in charge of the law enforcement detail at the Capitol.

After he left Fox News, Carlson used his new Twitter program called *Tucker on Twitter* to repeat some of the revelations gleaned from his Fox News interview with the Capitol Hill police chief.

Unfortunately, Fox News persisted in keeping that interview under wraps so that the general public could not confirm what Tucker Carlson was telling us.

Recently, however, Tucker Carlson figured out a way to get the last laugh. He was somehow able to convince the now retired Steven Sund to participate in a brand-new long-form interview with Tucker Carlson as part of Carlson's new Twitter program.

This new interview became an important news event. The Capitol Hill police chief confirmed all of the things Carlson had been telling us about the first interview.

Most importantly, Chief Sund confirmed that there were operatives of our government embedded in the crowd of January 6. In fact, Sund indicated that it would be highly unusual for something like January 6 to occur without undercover agents working the crowd.

Most stunningly, Sund revealed that federal authorities had access to pre-insurrection intelligence that easily predicted the chaos that ensued on that day. In this Twitter interview, Sund is filled with anger that this intelligence was not shared with him, therefore stripping him of the opportunity to be properly prepared.

Sund explains that he could easily have marshaled additional resources to prevent protester entry into the Capitol building if this intelligence would've been shared with him ahead of time.

He also explained that there were National Guard troops available nearby the capitol and that his request for their assistance at the time of the melee was denied. He expresses concern that perhaps federal authorities were intentionally trying to limit his ability to control the crowds.

Steven Sund said he found it especially galling that military assets were sent to the homes of the military brass in Washington as a precautionary measure to protect the generals. While that was happening, his request for additional assets was continuously denied until it was too late and the Capitol building had been breached.

Sund is completely incredulous when he tells Carlson that National Guard troops were finally deployed from a nearby Washington Armory at 6 PM on January 6 long after the need for those troops had disappeared.

He found it almost laughable that a National Guard division located in New Jersey traveled to Washington to assist him after he circulated an urgent message for mutual aid as the protesters became more threatening.

Capitol Hill Police Chief Steven Sund sat for a Tucker interview, twice.

The New Jersey national guardsmen arrived too late in the day to offer any real assistance but unbelievably they showed up on the scene before the National Guard located in the District of Columbia arrived.

The Steven Sund Twitter interview was a real "in-your-face" blow to the people at Fox News because Tucker Carlson had outsmarted his former employer at their own game.

Fox figured they could destroy Carlson's credibility by keeping the original interview under wraps so that none of Carlson's comments about the interview could be confirmed.

Fox didn't count on the fact that Carlson was determined to bring out the truth even if that meant having Steven Sund sit for a second interview on Carlson's new Twitter format. Fox wrongly concluded that Carlson would not be able to get Sund to participate in a second interview.

They were wrong. And as a result, they were humiliated.

Carlson still wasn't done in striking back at Fox News because he had another exciting plan.

Carlson would've been content to go quietly into the night and pursue his own Twitter program without causing harm to his former employer.

But Carlson realized Fox News was pursuing a scorched-earth attitude toward him by trying to embarrass him with the various out-takes. It also did not enhance Carlson's view of Fox when Fox contractors descended upon Carlson's home studio in Maine and stripped it of all the technical equipment needed to do broadcast.

The equipment certainly was owned by Fox but they knew that Carlson could easily rebuild that studio in just a matter of days. There was no reason to denude that studio other than to express public contempt against Carlson.

Not smart.

That's why Carlson put into place a surprise way to cause further heartburn for the Fox News Corporation.

Fox News spent millions of dollars promoting the very first Republican Primary Presidential debate in Milwaukee Wisconsin scheduled for August 22, 2023.

The world was full of anticipation at this very first opportunity to see eight Republican Presidential candidates debating each other before the first Republican primary.

Donald Trump had previously announced that he would not participate in this debate because he saw no benefit to appearing on stage with competitors so far behind Trump in the polls that Trump would diminish himself with a debate appearance.

Fox News was disappointed in that but also realized that the debate would be an exciting ratings success even without Trump.

Public eagerness for the debate began to build to an almost fever pitch when Tucker with the help of Donald Trump lowered the boom on this event.

Tucker Carlson conducted a live interview with Donald Trump on his twitter program exactly *simultaneous with the debate*. When the debate started, Carlson's interview with Trump started as well.

You can imagine what happened. Trump is always a lightning rod for attention but if you combine Trump with Carlson for a live interview, you have the formula to capture viewers in unprecedented numbers.

And that's exactly what happened.

The Fox Republican debate was somewhat interesting but was a ratings disappointment because the real excitement was happening in Tucker Carlson's newly rebuilt home studio. Trump did not disappoint and Carlson did not disappoint.

Tucker Carlson's interview with Trump on Twitter

garnered somewhere in the neighborhood of 140 million views while the Fox News debate in Milwaukee generated an audience of around 12 million.

What was supposed to be an audience bonanza for the Fox News Corporation turned into one of the major cable news disasters of all time.

As time marches forward, it is suspected that Fox News, now brought to its knees by the wily machinations of Tucker Carlson, will soon sign a formal settlement agreement with Carlson.

The ratings at Fox News have generally fallen into the toilet while Tucker Carlson continues to emerge as bigger and more important than ever before.

Many years ago, a margarine company distributed a TV commercial that warned "it's not nice to mess with Mother Nature."

Maybe now Fox News has learned something itself.

It's not nice to mess with Tucker Carlson.

ALSO BY DAVID LYNCH

Fat Tony, as Mayor, has a vise grip on all political and business activity in this town. Full of racism and corruption, his political machine operates with impunity. Accepting bribes and using the police to abuse black citizens who dare enter the community has been a winning formula for this crooked mayor anticipating reelection in this mostly white enclave.

Combine that with the mayor's Mafia connections and its clear taking on the Fat Tony mob could be hazardous to one's health. Despite this, an idealistic young attorney challenges him in the next mayor's race. The naïve newcomer faces destruction of his income, his family, and maybe even his life as this thriller crescendos in that fateful November election night. Everything rides on the election result.

You will cheer the challenger's successes and bite your nails as he faces down the threats... if only he can hang on until the bitter end. He's losing his confidence and his courage as the clock clicks down to this unbelievable ending.

The last few chapters race at blurring speed as the reader's adrenaline gets the heart pumping toward an amazing climax.

The best final three chapters in American literature!

ABOUT THE AUTHOR

David Lynch's career has been an exciting back and forth between government service and media.

A graduate of Georgetown University Law School, he began as a municipal prosecutor for the City of Cleveland where he learned about the ugly underbelly of the inner city. It also taught him a thing or two about politics and before you knew it, he was elected Mayor of the City of Euclid, Ohio at the tender age of 30.

He was subsequently named the best young mayor in America by the United States Junior Chamber of Commerce. President Bill Clinton invited him to the oval office for a one-on-one conference.

He then became the political commentator for the NBC

and Fox news affiliates in Cleveland. This was followed by syndication of *Live! With David Lynch* on the WB network.

On the writing end of things, his popular *Lynch Pen* column was a fan favorite in the Buckeye state. His most recent national television appearance featured his interview on *Fox and Friends*. *Tough Mother Tucker* is Lynch's second book.

David resides in Concord, Ohio with his wife Nancy, who he met in High School, both in a production of *My Fair Lady*. They have three children, Scott, Bridget, and Colleen.